Saxophone Exam Pack

ABRSM Grade 1

Selected from the 2018–2021 syllabus

Name

C000017062

Date of exam

Contents

page

Consultant Editor for ABRSM: David Blackwell
Footnotes: Anthony Burton

Other pieces for Grade 1

Alternative pieces for E♭ and B♭ saxophones are listed in the piano accompaniment booklet.

First published in 2017 by ABRSM (Publishing) Ltd,
a wholly owned subsidiary of ABRSM, 4 London Wall Place,
London EC2Y 5AU, United Kingdom
© 2017 by The Associated Board of the Royal Schools of Music
Distributed worldwide by Oxford University Press

Music origination by Julia Bovee and Katie Johnston (Sight-reading)
Cover by Kate Benjamin & Andy Potts
Printed in England by Halstan & Co. Ltd, Amersham, Bucks.,
on materials from sustainable sources.
Reprinted in 2017

A:1

Fine Knacks for Ladies

from *The Second Booke of Songs or Ayres*

Arranged by Ian Denley

John Dowland
(1563–1626)

John Dowland was one of the most famous English musicians of his time, as a performer on the lute (forerunner of the guitar) and a composer. He published several volumes of 'Songs or Ayres', mostly for voice and lute; this song comes from the second book, which dates from 1600. In this song, a man takes on the character of a street trader to offer his girlfriend, in bars 1–4, 'Fine knacks for ladies, cheap, choice, brave and new' (a 'knack' was an inexpensive trinket); but he insists, from bar 17, 'Though all my wares be trash the heart is true.'

© 2001 by The Associated Board of the Royal Schools of Music
Reproduced from *Time Pieces for E flat Saxophone*, Volume 1 and *Time Pieces for B flat Saxophone*, Volume 1, selected and arranged by Ian Denley (ABRSM)

March

from *Scipio*, HWV 20

Arranged by Nicholas Scott-Burt

G. F. Handel
(1685–1759)

Handel first came to England in 1711 as a composer of Italian operas, and over the next three decades he wrote well over 30 operas for the London stage. One of them was *Scipione*, or *Scipio*, first produced in 1726. Its opening scene begins with an orchestral March accompanying the arrival of the Roman conqueror Scipio in the Spanish port of New Carthage. This bright, lively March soon became well known as an independent piece.

Skye Boat Song

Arranged by Alan Bullard

Trad. Scottish

The *Skye Boat Song* first appeared in a collection published in 1884 called *Songs of the North*, edited by Sir Harold Boulton and Annie MacLeod. The words by Boulton refer to the time of the second Jacobite rebellion against English rule in Scotland in 1745/46 and tell the story of how the leader of the rebellion, known as 'Bonny Prince Charlie' or 'the Young Pretender', was rowed to the Isle of Skye following his defeat at the Battle of Culloden. These words are fitted to a tune adapted by MacLeod from a traditional Scottish rowing song. The recurring rhythm of bars 5, 7, etc. has a lilting Scottish quality, and suggests the gentle movement of the oars.

7ᵗʰ Dec

The Little Sandman

Sandmännchen

No. 4 from *Volks-Kinderlieder*, WoO 31

B:1

Arranged by Nancy Litten

Johannes Brahms
(1833–97)

'The Little Sandman' is a German folk song about the mythical character who visits sleeping children and sprinkles magic sand on their eyes to bring them pleasant dreams. Brahms arranged it as part of a set of *Folk Songs for Children*, published in 1858 with a dedication to the young children of his friends Robert and Clara Schumann. This arrangement preserves the melody of the song and also Brahms's piano part, adding an introduction and leaving out Brahms's piano conclusion.

B:2

Jazz Music for Beetles

Ned Bennett
(born 1966)

Ned Bennett is a jazz saxophonist based in south London, and has composed and arranged for many jazz and classical soloists and groups. He says of his *Jazz Music for Beetles*: 'Swing this one, but follow the slur pattern, from offbeats to onbeats. Make the most of the dynamics for full effect. A heavy groove like this is typical of pieces by Art Blakey and the Jazz Messengers with Cannonball Adderley on alto. Note how the piano has very little variety, but sets up a rhythmic feel which is infectious.'

On the Ball

B:3

James Rae
(born 1957)

Bright shuffle feel ♩ = c.120

James Rae is a clarinettist and saxophonist based in the London area, the leader of the Phoenix Saxophone Quartet, and also a teacher and a prolific composer. His *On the Ball* comes from a collection of pieces by various composers with football-related titles. He says that it should be 'played with a cool, rhythmic feel in order to bring out the "laid-back" character of the music. A strong sense of pulse is essential to synchronize the saxophone line with the shuffle-style accompaniment.'

© Gumbles Publications 2017
Taken from *Final Whistle!* (Rae/Bullard/Gumbley). Available from gumblespublications.co.uk.

C:1

Swinging Circles

No. 4 from *Blues for One*, Vol. 1

Ian Morrison
(born 1965)

Ian Morrison teaches the saxophone, conducts two wind ensembles, and plays saxophone and bass guitar in several groups. He is also a prolific composer and arranger for various instruments and groups. His 'Swinging Circles' is in jazz waltz time, as if over a regular three-in-a-bar accompaniment. The markings for slurred, tenuto and staccato notes all help to give the piece its character.

Gossip

from *35 Melodic Studies for Saxophone*

Graham Salter

Graham Salter is an experienced oboist who has played in almost every major orchestra in London and the United Kingdom. This piece comes from a collection of studies for oboe or saxophone – two instruments with similar ranges – designed 'to develop control and expressive playing'.

Sweet Nightingale

Arranged by Gordon Lewin

Trad. English

Sweet Nightingale is a folk song from Cornwall, in the south-west of England. It is often sung by choirs. The words of the first verse, in one of many traditional versions, are:

> My sweetheart come along,
> Don't you hear the fond song,
> The sweet notes of the nightingale flow?
> Don't you hear the fond tale
> Of the sweet nightingale,
> As she sings in the valley below,
> As she sings in the valley below?

The word 'below' is sung the first time to the whole phrase from the end of bar 14 to the start of bar 18.

© 1989 by The Associated Board of the Royal Schools of Music
Reproduced from Gordon Lewin: *Starters for Saxophone* (ABRSM)

Scales and arpeggios

SCALES

from memory
tongued *and* slurred

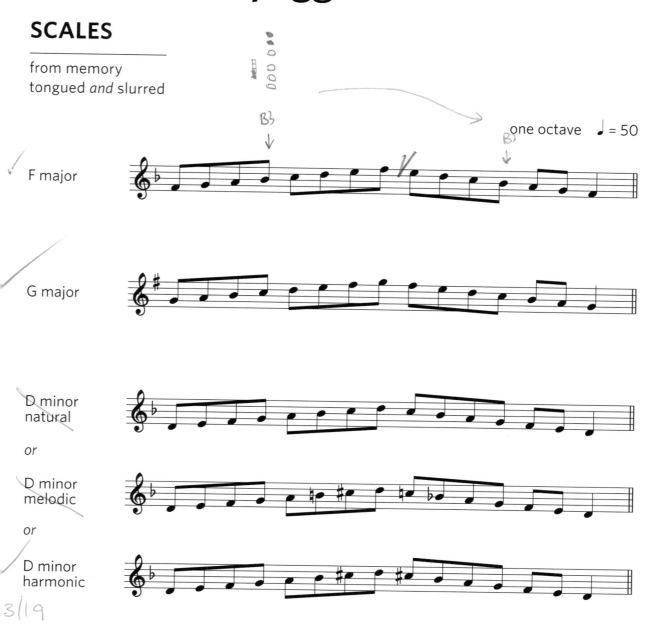

F major

G major

D minor
natural

or

D minor
melodic

or

D minor
harmonic

3/19

Scales and arpeggios

ARPEGGIOS

from memory
tongued *and* slurred

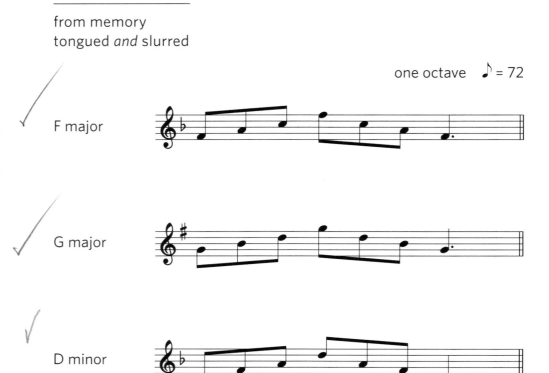

one octave   ♪ = 72

F major

G major

D minor

Sight-reading

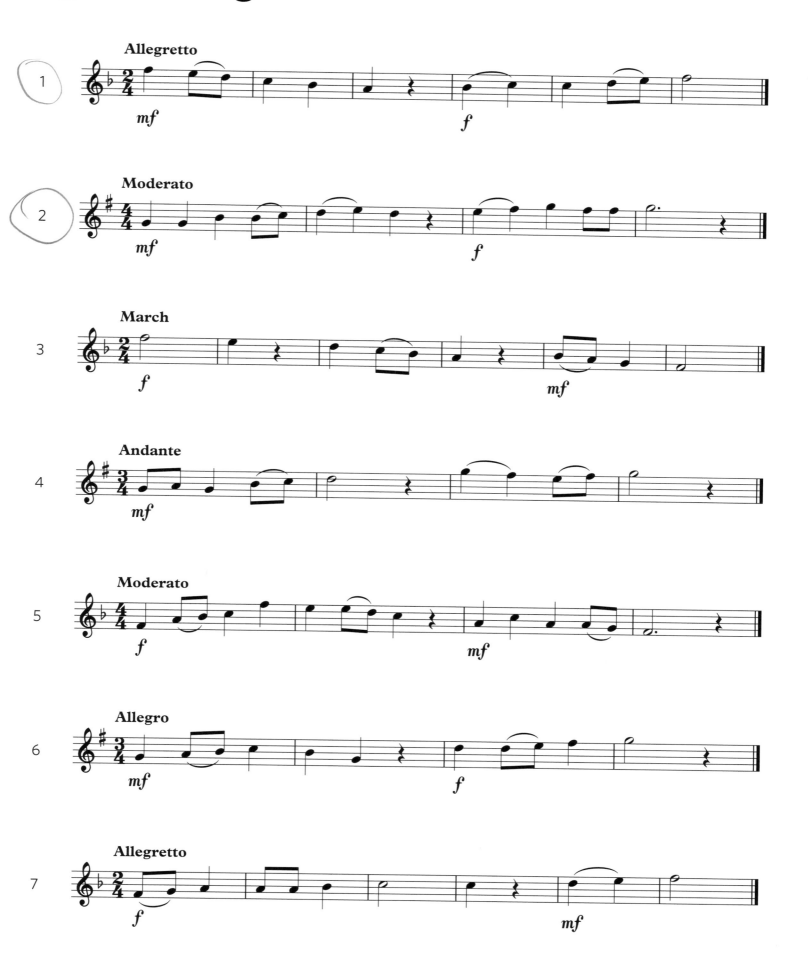

Sight-reading

Sight-reading

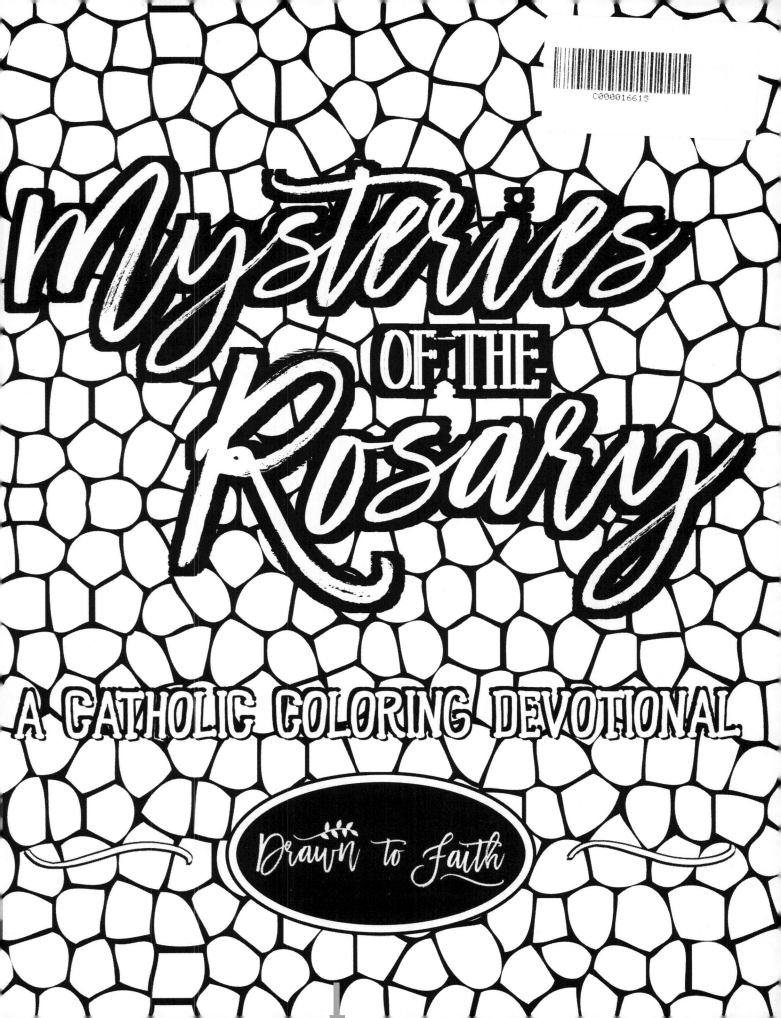

Illustrated by Maryna

ISBN-13: 978-1-945888-41-0
ISBN-10: 1-945888-41-5

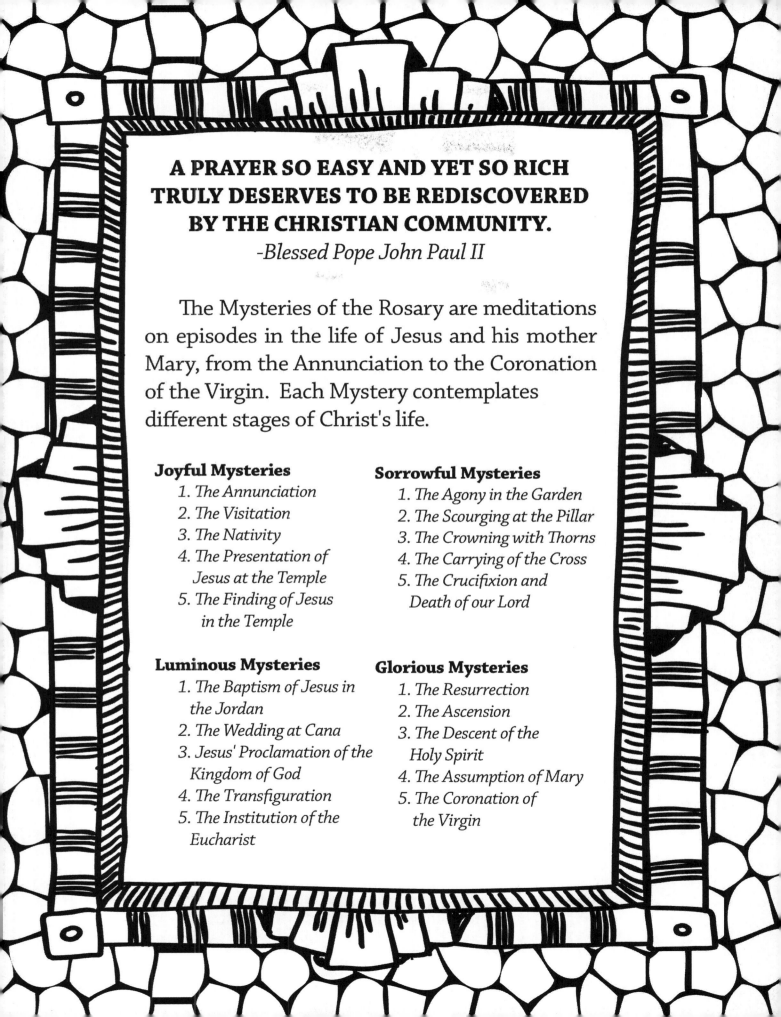

A PRAYER SO EASY AND YET SO RICH TRULY DESERVES TO BE REDISCOVERED BY THE CHRISTIAN COMMUNITY.

-Blessed Pope John Paul II

The Mysteries of the Rosary are meditations on episodes in the life of Jesus and his mother Mary, from the Annunciation to the Coronation of the Virgin. Each Mystery contemplates different stages of Christ's life.

Joyful Mysteries

1. *The Annunciation*
2. *The Visitation*
3. *The Nativity*
4. *The Presentation of Jesus at the Temple*
5. *The Finding of Jesus in the Temple*

Sorrowful Mysteries

1. *The Agony in the Garden*
2. *The Scourging at the Pillar*
3. *The Crowning with Thorns*
4. *The Carrying of the Cross*
5. *The Crucifixion and Death of our Lord*

Luminous Mysteries

1. *The Baptism of Jesus in the Jordan*
2. *The Wedding at Cana*
3. *Jesus' Proclamation of the Kingdom of God*
4. *The Transfiguration*
5. *The Institution of the Eucharist*

Glorious Mysteries

1. *The Resurrection*
2. *The Ascension*
3. *The Descent of the Holy Spirit*
4. *The Assumption of Mary*
5. *The Coronation of the Virgin*

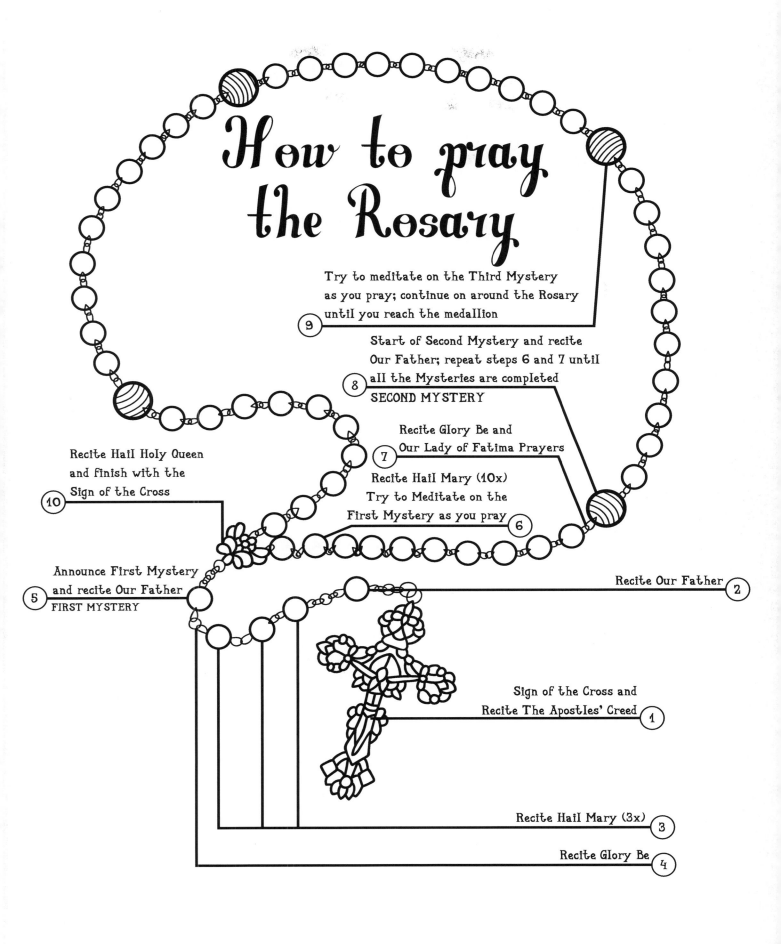

How to pray the Rosary

Try to meditate on the Third Mystery as you pray; continue on around the Rosary until you reach the medallion — 9

Start of Second Mystery and recite Our Father; repeat steps 6 and 7 until all the Mysteries are completed — 8
SECOND MYSTERY

Recite Glory Be and Our Lady of Fatima Prayers — 7

Recite Hail Mary (10x)
Try to Meditate on the First Mystery as you pray — 6

Recite Hail Holy Queen and finish with the Sign of the Cross — 10

Announce First Mystery and recite Our Father — 5
FIRST MYSTERY

Recite Our Father — 2

Sign of the Cross and Recite The Apostles' Creed — 1

Recite Hail Mary (3x) — 3

Recite Glory Be — 4

the Apostles' Creed

I BELIEVE IN GOD,
THE FATHER ALMIGHTY,
CREATOR OF HEAVEN AND EARTH,
AND IN JESUS CHRIST, HIS ONLY SON, OUR LORD,
WHO WAS CONCEIVED BY THE HOLY SPIRIT,
BORN OF THE VIRGIN MARY,
SUFFERED UNDER PONTIUS PILATE,
WAS CRUCIFIED, DIED AND WAS BURIED:
HE DESCENDED INTO HELL:
ON THE THIRD DAY HE ROSE AGAIN FROM THE DEAD:
HE ASCENDED INTO HEAVEN,
AND IS SEATED AT THE RIGHT HAND OF GOD THE FATHER
ALMIGHTY:
FROM THERE HE WILL COME TO JUDGE THE LIVING AND
THE DEAD.
I BELIEVE IN THE HOLY SPIRIT,
THE HOLY CATHOLIC CHURCH,
THE COMMUNION OF SAINTS,
THE FORGIVENESS OF SINS,
THE RESURRECTION OF THE BODY,
AND LIFE EVERLASTING. AMEN.

Our Father
(THE LORD'S PRAYER)

OUR FATHER
WHO ART IN HEAVEN,
HALLOWED BE THY NAME.
THY KINGDOM COME:
THY WILL BE DONE ON EARTH AS IT IS IN HEAVEN.
GIVE US THIS DAY OUR DAILY BREAD
AND FORGIVE US OUR TRESPASSES
AS WE FORGIVE THOSE WHO TRESPASS AGAINST US.
AND LEAD US NOT INTO TEMPTATION,
BUT DELIVER US FROM EVIL.
AMEN.

Glory Be

(OR THE GLORIA)

GLORY BE TO THE FATHER
AND TO THE SON
AND TO THE HOLY SPIRIT,
AS IT WAS IN THE BEGINNING,
IS NOW,
AND EVER SHALL BE,
WORLD WITHOUT END. AMEN.

Hail Holy Queen

(OR THE SALVE REGINA)

HAIL, HOLY QUEEN, MOTHER OF MERCY,
OUR LIFE, OUR SWEETNESS AND OUR HOPE!
TO YOU DO WE CRY,
POOR BANISHED CHILDREN OF EVE:
TO YOU DO WE SEND UP OUR SIGHS,
MOURNING AND WEEPING IN THIS VALLEY OF TEARS.
TURN THEN, O MOST GRACIOUS ADVOCATE,
YOUR EYES OF MERCY TOWARD US,
AND AFTER THIS EXILE,
SHOW US THE BLESSED FRUIT OF YOUR WOMB, JESUS.
O CLEMENT, O LOVING, O SWEET VIRGIN MARY.
V. PRAY FOR US, O HOLY MOTHER OF GOD.
R. THAT WE MAY BE MADE WORTHY OF THE PROMISES
OF CHRIST. AMEN.

Prayer of Our Lady of Fatima,

(DECADE PRAYER)

O MY JESUS, FORGIVE US OUR SINS, SAVE US FROM THE FIRES OF HELL, LEAD ALL SOULS TO HEAVEN, ESPECIALLY THOSE WHO ARE IN MOST NEED OF YOUR MERCY.

Concluding Prayer

O GOD, WHOSE ONLY BEGOTTEN SON, BY WHOSE LIFE, DEATH AND RESURRECTION, HAS PURCHASED FOR US THE REWARDS OF ETERNAL LIFE.

GRANT, WE BESEECH THEE, THAT BY MEDITATING UPON THESE MYSTERIES OF THE MOST HOLY ROSARY OF THE BLESSED VIRGIN MARY, THAT WE MAY IMITATE WHAT THEY CONTAIN AND OBTAIN WHAT THEY PROMISE, THROUGH CHRIST OUR LORD. AMEN.

FIRST JOYFUL MYSTERY:

The Annunciation

_____
_____
_____
_____
_____
_____
_____
_____
_____
_____
_____

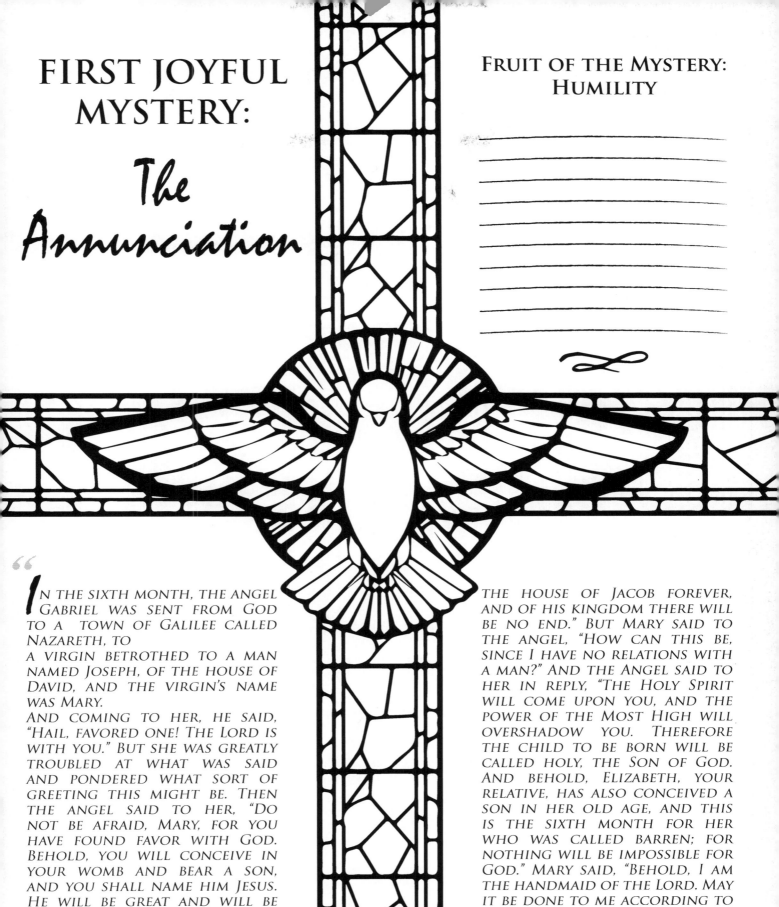

"IN THE SIXTH MONTH, THE ANGEL GABRIEL WAS SENT FROM GOD TO A TOWN OF GALILEE CALLED NAZARETH, TO A VIRGIN BETROTHED TO A MAN NAMED JOSEPH, OF THE HOUSE OF DAVID, AND THE VIRGIN'S NAME WAS MARY. AND COMING TO HER, HE SAID, "HAIL, FAVORED ONE! THE LORD IS WITH YOU." BUT SHE WAS GREATLY TROUBLED AT WHAT WAS SAID AND PONDERED WHAT SORT OF GREETING THIS MIGHT BE. THEN THE ANGEL SAID TO HER, "DO NOT BE AFRAID, MARY, FOR YOU HAVE FOUND FAVOR WITH GOD. BEHOLD, YOU WILL CONCEIVE IN YOUR WOMB AND BEAR A SON, AND YOU SHALL NAME HIM JESUS. HE WILL BE GREAT AND WILL BE CALLED SON OF THE MOST HIGH, AND THE LORD GOD WILL GIVE HIM THE THRONE OF DAVID HIS FATHER, AND HE WILL RULE OVER THE HOUSE OF JACOB FOREVER, AND OF HIS KINGDOM THERE WILL BE NO END." BUT MARY SAID TO THE ANGEL, "HOW CAN THIS BE, SINCE I HAVE NO RELATIONS WITH A MAN?" AND THE ANGEL SAID TO HER IN REPLY, "THE HOLY SPIRIT WILL COME UPON YOU, AND THE POWER OF THE MOST HIGH WILL OVERSHADOW YOU. THEREFORE THE CHILD TO BE BORN WILL BE CALLED HOLY, THE SON OF GOD. AND BEHOLD, ELIZABETH, YOUR RELATIVE, HAS ALSO CONCEIVED A SON IN HER OLD AGE, AND THIS IS THE SIXTH MONTH FOR HER WHO WAS CALLED BARREN; FOR NOTHING WILL BE IMPOSSIBLE FOR GOD." MARY SAID, "BEHOLD, I AM THE HANDMAID OF THE LORD. MAY IT BE DONE TO ME ACCORDING TO YOUR WORD." THEN THE ANGEL DEPARTED FROM HER'"

LUKE 1:26-38

First Joyful Mystery: The Annunciation

SECOND JOYFUL MYSTERY:

The Visitation

FRUIT OF THE MYSTERY:
LOVE OF NEIGHBORS

_____
_____
_____
_____
_____
_____
_____
_____
_____
_____

"DURING THOSE DAYS MARY SET OUT AND TRAVELED TO THE HILL COUNTRY IN HASTE TO A TOWN OF JUDAH, WHERE SHE ENTERED THE HOUSE OF ZECHARIAH AND GREETED ELIZABETH. WHEN ELIZABETH HEARD MARY'S GREETING, THE INFANT LEAPED IN HER WOMB, AND ELIZABETH, FILLED WITH THE HOLY SPIRIT, CRIED OUT IN A LOUD VOICE AND SAID, "MOST BLESSED ARE YOU AMONG WOMEN, AND BLESSED IS THE FRUIT OF YOUR WOMB."

LUKE 1:39-4

"AND MARY SAID: "MY SOUL MAGNIFIES THE LORD. AND MY SPIRIT LEAPS FOR JOY IN GOD MY SAVIOR. FOR HE HAS LOOKED WITH FAVOR ON THE HUMILITY OF HIS HANDMAID. FOR BEHOLD, FROM THIS TIME, ALL GENERATIONS SHALL CALL ME BLESSED. FOR HE WHO IS GREAT HAS DONE GREAT THINGS FOR ME, AND HOLY IS HIS NAME."

LUKE 1:46-49

Second Joyful Mystery:
The Visitation

THIRD JOYFUL MYSTERY:

The Nativity

_____
_____
_____
_____
_____
_____
_____
_____
_____

"AND IT HAPPENED IN THOSE DAYS THAT A DECREE WENT OUT FROM CAESAR AUGUSTUS, SO THAT THE WHOLE WORLD WOULD BE ENROLLED. THIS WAS THE FIRST ENROLLMENT; IT WAS MADE BY THE RULER OF SYRIA, QUIRINIUS. AND ALL WENT TO BE DECLARED, EACH ONE TO HIS OWN CITY. THEN JOSEPH ALSO ASCENDED FROM GALILEE, FROM THE CITY OF NAZARETH, INTO JUDEA, TO THE CITY OF DAVID, WHICH IS CALLED BETHLEHEM, BECAUSE HE WAS OF THE HOUSE AND FAMILY OF DAVID, IN ORDER TO BE DECLARED, WITH MARY HIS ESPOUSED WIFE, WHO WAS WITH CHILD. THEN IT HAPPENED THAT, WHILE THEY WERE THERE, THE DAYS WERE COMPLETED, SO THAT SHE WOULD GIVE BIRTH. AND SHE BROUGHT FORTH HER FIRSTBORN SON. AND SHE WRAPPED HIM IN SWADDLING CLOTHES AND LAID HIM IN A MANGER, BECAUSE THERE WAS NO ROOM FOR THEM AT THE INN. AND THERE WERE SHEPHERDS IN THE SAME REGION, BEING VIGILANT AND KEEPING WATCH IN THE NIGHT OVER THEIR FLOCK. AND BEHOLD, AN ANGEL OF THE LORD STOOD NEAR THEM, AND THE BRIGHTNESS OF GOD SHONE AROUND THEM, AND THEY WERE STRUCK WITH A GREAT FEAR. AND THE ANGEL SAID TO THEM: "DO NOT BE AFRAID. FOR, BEHOLD, I PROCLAIM TO YOU A GREAT JOY, WHICH WILL BE FOR ALL THE PEOPLE. FOR TODAY A SAVIOR HAS BEEN BORN FOR YOU IN THE CITY OF DAVID: HE IS CHRIST THE LORD. AND THIS WILL BE A SIGN FOR YOU: YOU WILL FIND THE INFANT WRAPPED IN SWADDLING CLOTHES AND LYING IN A MANGER." AND SUDDENLY THERE WAS WITH THE ANGEL A MULTITUDE OF THE CELESTIAL ARMY, PRAISING GOD AND SAYING, "GLORY TO GOD IN THE HIGHEST, AND ON EARTH PEACE TO MEN OF GOOD WILL."

LUKE 2:1-14

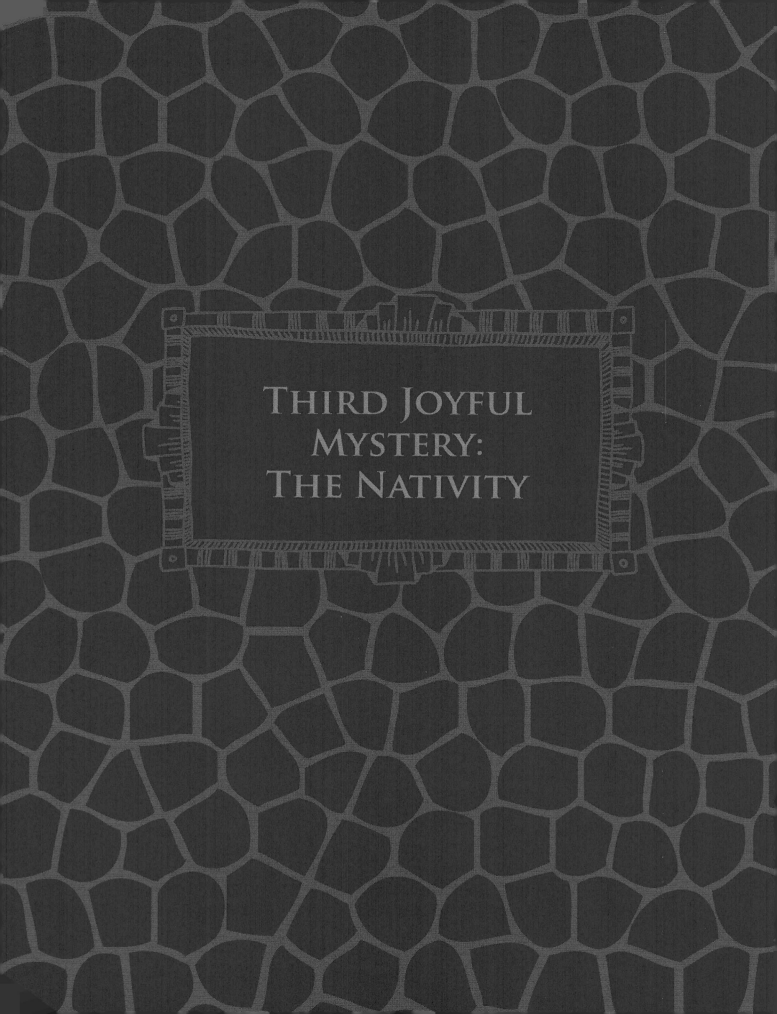

THIRD JOYFUL MYSTERY: THE NATIVITY

FOURTH JOYFUL MYSTERY:

The Presentation of Jesus in the Temple

"WHEN EIGHT DAYS WERE COMPLETED FOR HIS CIRCUMCISION, HE WAS NAMED JESUS, THE NAME GIVEN HIM BY THE ANGEL BEFORE HE WAS CONCEIVED IN THE WOMB. WHEN THE DAYS WERE COMPLETED FOR THEIR PURIFICATION ACCORDING TO THE LAW OF MOSES, THEY TOOK HIM UP TO JERUSALEM TO PRESENT HIM TO THE LORD, JUST AS IT IS WRITTEN IN THE LAW OF THE LORD "EVERY MALE THAT OPENS THE WOMB SHALL BE CONSECRATED TO THE LORD," AND TO OFFER THE SACRIFICE OF "A PAIR OF TURTLEDOVES OR TWO YOUNG PIGEONS," IN ACCORDANCE WITH THE DICTATE IN THE LAW OF THE LORD"

LUKE 2:21-24

"AND BEHOLD, THERE WAS A MAN IN JERUSALEM, WHOSE NAME WAS SIMEON, AND THIS MAN WAS JUST AND GOD-FEARING, AWAITING THE CONSOLATION OF ISRAEL. AND THE HOLY SPIRIT WAS WITH HIM. AND HE HAD RECEIVED AN ANSWER FROM THE HOLY SPIRIT: THAT HE WOULD NOT SEE HIS OWN DEATH BEFORE HE HAD SEEN THE CHRIST OF THE LORD. AND HE WENT WITH THE SPIRIT TO THE TEMPLE. AND WHEN THE CHILD JESUS WAS BROUGHT IN BY HIS PARENTS, IN ORDER TO ACT ON HIS BEHALF ACCORDING TO THE CUSTOM OF THE LAW, HE ALSO TOOK HIM UP, INTO HIS ARMS, AND HE BLESSED GOD AND SAID: "NOW YOU MAY DISMISS YOUR SERVANT IN PEACE, O LORD, ACCORDING TO YOUR WORD. FOR MY EYES HAVE SEEN YOUR SALVATION, WHICH YOU HAVE PREPARED BEFORE THE FACE OF ALL PEOPLES: THE LIGHT OF REVELATION TO THE NATIONS AND THE GLORY OF YOUR PEOPLE ISRAEL.""

LUKE 2:25-32

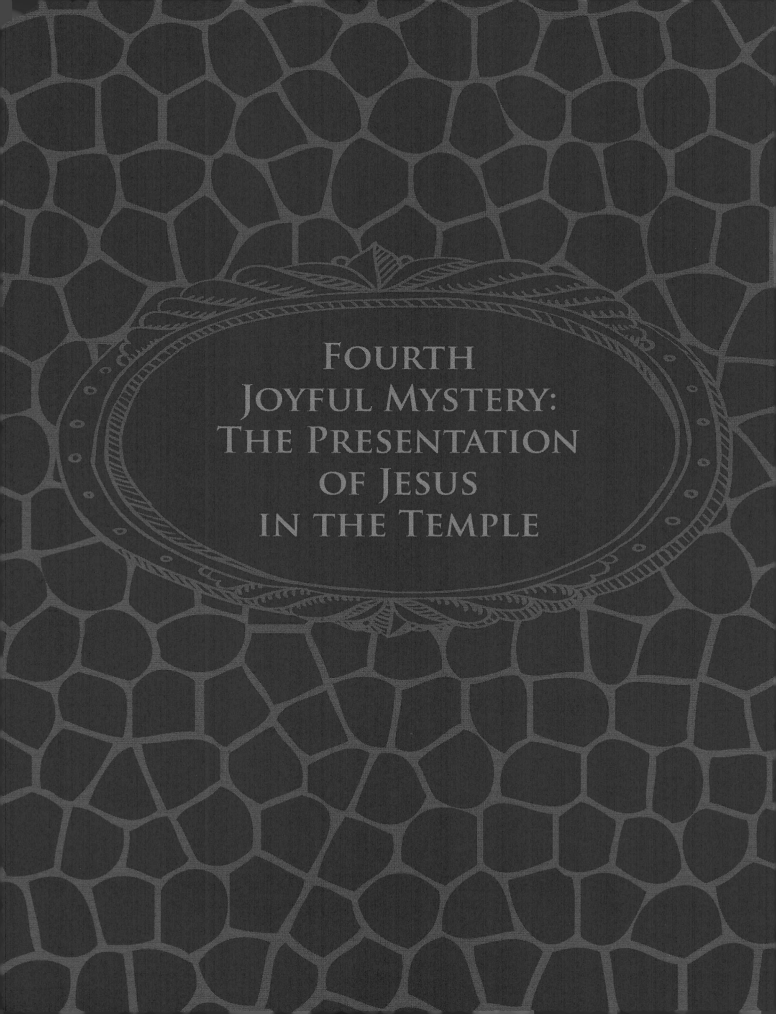

Fourth Joyful Mystery: The Presentation of Jesus in the Temple

FIFTH JOYFUL MYSTERY:

The Finding of Jesus in the Temple

"Now the child grew, and he was strengthened with the fullness of wisdom. And the grace of God was in him. And his parents went every year to Jerusalem, at the time of the solemnity of Passover. And when he had become twelve years old, they ascended to Jerusalem, according to the custom of the feast day. And having completed the days, when they returned, the boy Jesus remained in Jerusalem. And his parents did not realize this. But, supposing that he was in the company, they went a day's journey, seeking him among their relatives and acquaintances. And not finding him, they returned to Jerusalem, seeking him. And it happened that, after three days, they found him in the temple, sitting in the midst of the doctors, listening to them and questioning them.

But all who listened to him were astonished over his prudence and his responses. And upon seeing him, they wondered. And his mother said to him: "Son, why have you acted this way toward us? Behold, your father and I were seeking you in sorrow." And he said to them: "How is it that you were seeking me? For did you not know that it is necessary for me to be in these things which are of my Father?" And they did not understand the word that he spoke to them. And he descended with them and went to Nazareth. And he was subordinate to them. And his mother kept all these words in her heart. And Jesus advanced in wisdom, and in age, and in grace, with God and men. "

Luke 2:40-52

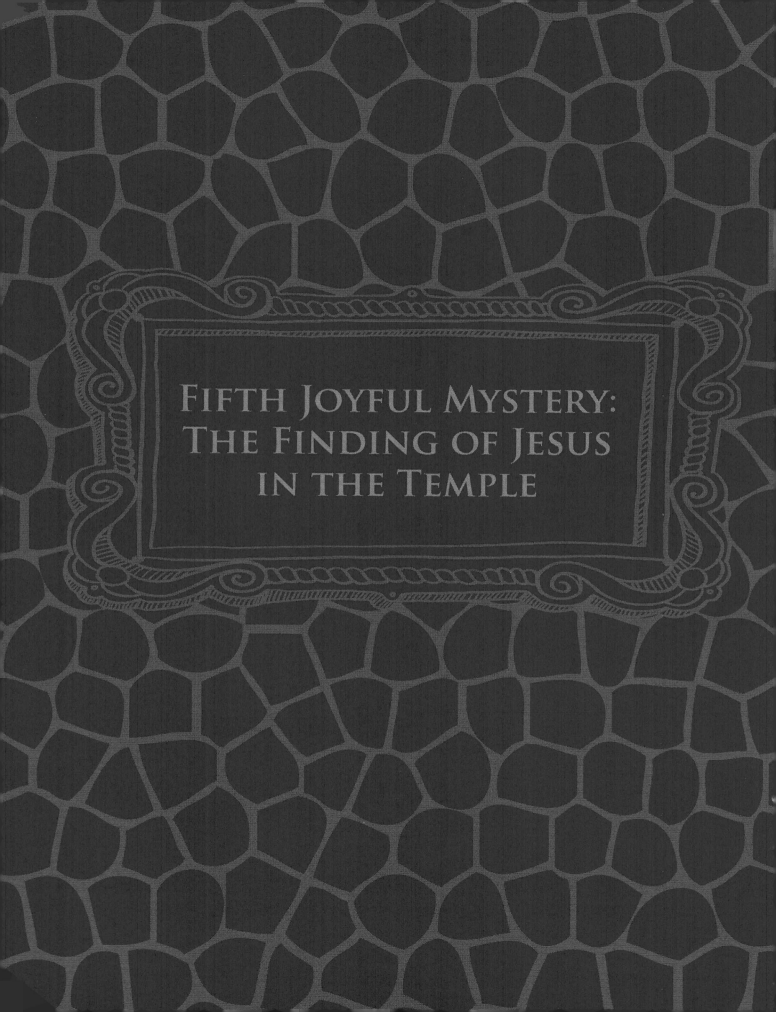

Fifth Joyful Mystery: The Finding of Jesus in the Temple

FIRST LUMINOUS MYSTERY:

The Baptism of Jesus in the Jordan

"AFTER JESUS WAS BAPTIZED, HE CAME UP FROM THE WATER AND BEHOLD, THE HEAVENS WERE OPENED [FOR HIM], AND HE SAW THE SPIRIT OF GOD DESCENDING LIKE A DOVE [AND] COMING UPON HIM. AND A VOICE CAME FROM THE HEAVENS, SAYING, "THIS IS MY BELOVED SON, WITH WHOM I AM WELL PLEASED.""

MATTHEW 3:16-17

"NOW IT HAPPENED THAT, WHEN ALL THE PEOPLE WERE BEING BAPTIZED, JESUS WAS BAPTIZED; AND AS HE WAS PRAYING, HEAVEN WAS OPENED. AND THE HOLY SPIRIT, IN A CORPORAL APPEARANCE LIKE A DOVE, DESCENDED UPON HIM. AND A VOICE CAME FROM HEAVEN: "YOU ARE MY BELOVED SON. IN YOU, I AM WELL PLEASED.""

LUKE 3:21-22

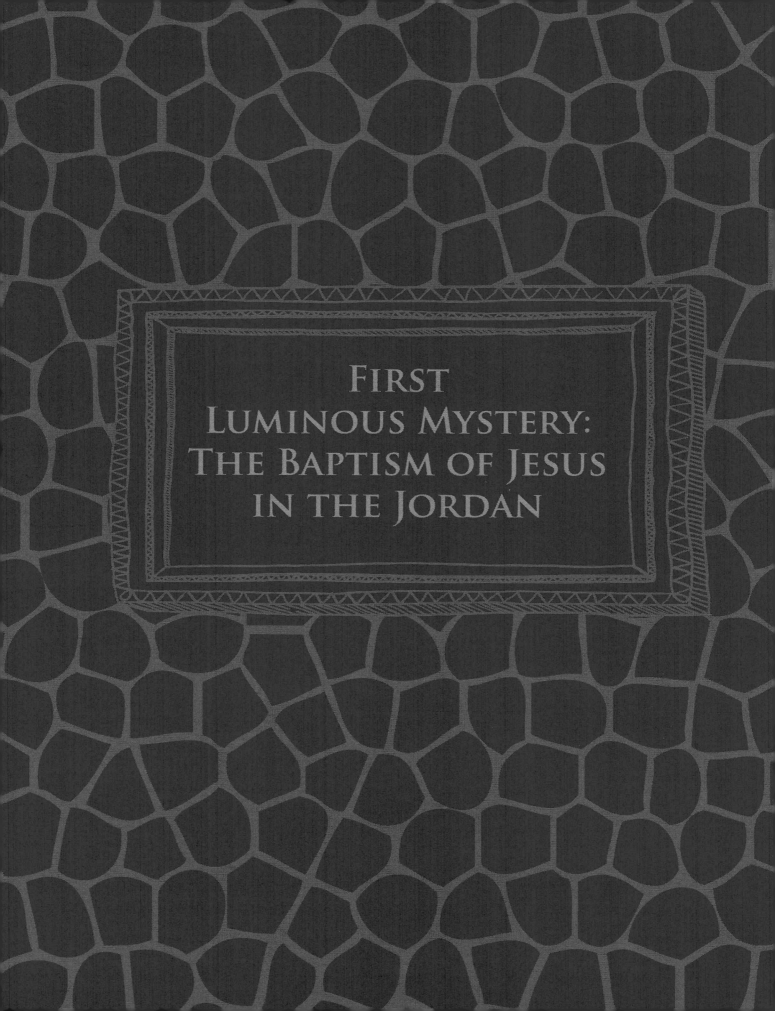

First Luminous Mystery: The Baptism of Jesus in the Jordan

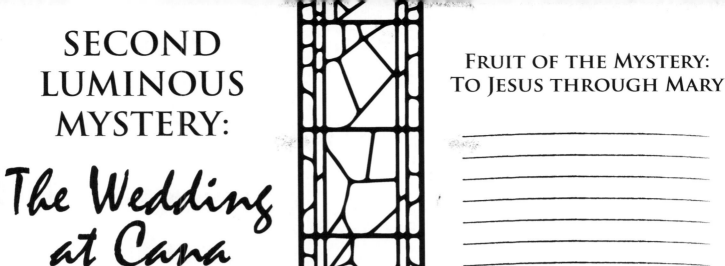

SECOND LUMINOUS MYSTERY:

The Wedding at Cana

"AND ON THE THIRD DAY, A WEDDING WAS HELD IN CANA OF GALILEE, AND THE MOTHER OF JESUS WAS THERE. NOW JESUS WAS ALSO INVITED TO THE WEDDING, WITH HIS DISCIPLES. AND WHEN THE WINE WAS FAILING, THE MOTHER OF JESUS SAID TO HIM, "THEY HAVE NO WINE." AND JESUS SAID TO HER: "WHAT IS THAT TO ME AND TO YOU, WOMAN? MY HOUR HAS NOT YET ARRIVED." HIS MOTHER SAID TO THE SERVANTS, "DO WHATEVER HE TELLS YOU." NOW IN THAT PLACE, THERE WERE SIX STONE WATER JARS, FOR THE PURIFICATION RITUAL OF THE JEWS, CONTAINING TWO OR THREE MEASURES EACH. JESUS SAID TO THEM, "FILL THE WATER JARS WITH WATER." AND THEY FILLED THEM TO THE VERY TOP. AND JESUS SAID TO THEM, "NOW DRAW FROM IT, AND CARRY IT TO THE CHIEF STEWARD OF THE FEAST." AND THEY TOOK IT TO HIM. THEN, WHEN THE CHIEF STEWARD HAD TASTED THE WATER MADE INTO WINE, SINCE HE DID NOT KNOW WHERE IT WAS FROM, FOR ONLY THE SERVANTS WHO HAD DRAWN THE WATER KNEW, THE CHIEF STEWARD CALLED THE GROOM, AND HE SAID TO HIM: "EVERY MAN OFFERS THE GOOD WINE FIRST, AND THEN, WHEN THEY HAVE BECOME INEBRIATED, HE OFFERS WHAT IS WORSE. BUT YOU HAVE KEPT THE GOOD WINE UNTIL NOW." THIS WAS THE BEGINNING OF THE SIGNS THAT JESUS ACCOMPLISHED IN CANA OF GALILEE, AND IT MANIFESTED HIS GLORY, AND HIS DISCIPLES BELIEVED IN HIM."

JOHN 2:1-11

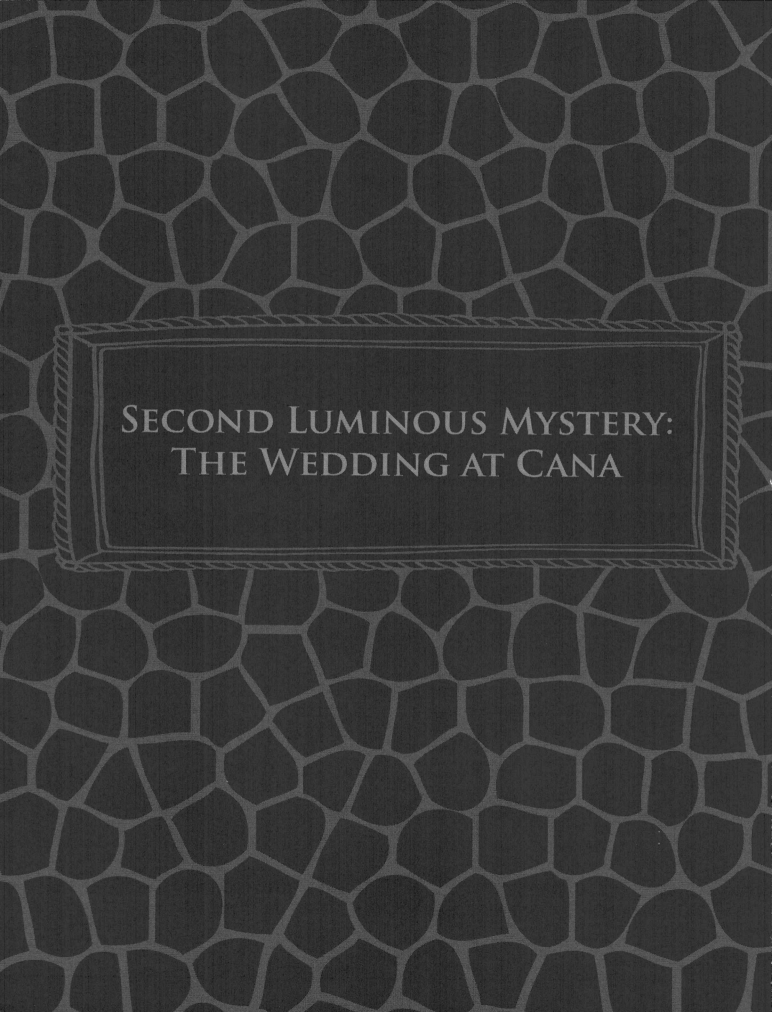

Second Luminous Mystery:
The Wedding at Cana

THIRD LUMINOUS MYSTERY:

Jesus' Proclamation of the Kingdom of God

"THIS IS THE TIME OF FULFILLMENT. THE KINGDOM OF GOD IS AT HAND. REPENT, AND BELIEVE IN THE GOSPEL."

MARK 1:15

"BLESSED ARE THE POOR IN SPIRIT, FOR THEIRS IS THE KINGDOM OF HEAVEN. BLESSED ARE YOU WHO MOURN, FOR THEY WILL BE COMFORTED. BLESSED ARE THE MEEK, FOR THEY WILL INHERIT THE LAND... BLESSED ARE THE MERCIFUL, FOR THEY WILL BE SHOWN MERCY"

MATTHEW 5:3-12

Third Luminous Mystery:
Jesus' Proclamation of the Kingdom of God

FOURTH LUMINOUS MYSTERY:

The Transfiguration

FRUIT OF THE MYSTERY: DESIRE FOR HOLINESS

_____
_____
_____
_____
_____
_____
_____
_____

"AND AFTER SIX DAYS, JESUS TOOK PETER AND JAMES AND HIS BROTHER JOHN, AND HE LED THEM ONTO A LOFTY MOUNTAIN SEPARATELY. AND HE WAS TRANSFIGURED BEFORE THEM. AND HIS FACE SHINED BRIGHTLY LIKE THE SUN. AND HIS GARMENTS WERE MADE WHITE LIKE SNOW. AND BEHOLD, THERE APPEARED TO THEM MOSES AND ELIJAH, SPEAKING WITH HIM. AND PETER RESPONDED BY SAYING TO JESUS: "LORD, IT IS GOOD FOR US TO BE HERE. IF YOU ARE WILLING, LET US MAKE THREE TABERNACLES HERE, ONE FOR YOU, ONE FOR MOSES, AND ONE FOR ELIJAH." AND WHILE HE WAS STILL SPEAKING, BEHOLD, A SHINING CLOUD OVERSHADOWED THEM. AND BEHOLD, THERE WAS A VOICE FROM THE CLOUD, SAYING: "THIS IS MY BELOVED SON, WITH WHOM I AM WELL PLEASED. LISTEN TO HIM." AND THE DISCIPLES, HEARING THIS, FELL PRONE ON THEIR FACE, AND THEY WERE VERY AFRAID. AND JESUS DREW NEAR AND TOUCHED THEM. AND HE SAID TO THEM, "RISE UP AND DO NOT BE AFRAID." AND LIFTING UP THEIR EYES, THEY SAW NO ONE, EXCEPT JESUS ALONE. AND AS THEY WERE DESCENDING FROM THE MOUNTAIN, JESUS INSTRUCTED THEM, SAYING, "TELL NO ONE ABOUT THE VISION, UNTIL THE SON OF MAN HAS RISEN FROM THE DEAD.""

MATTHEW 17:1-9

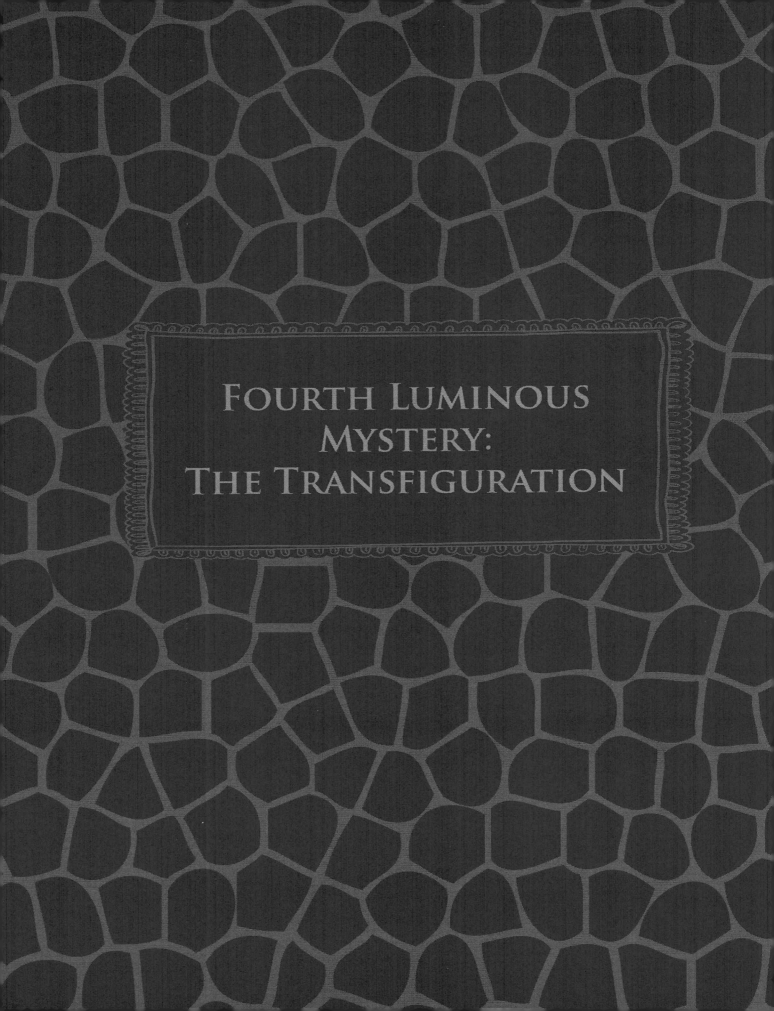

Fourth Luminous Mystery: The Transfiguration

FIFTH LUMINOUS MYSTERY:
The Institution of the Eucharist

_____
_____
_____
_____
_____
_____
_____
_____
_____
_____
_____

"Now while they were eating the meal, Jesus took bread, and he blessed and broke and gave it to his disciples, and he said: "Take and eat. This is my body." And taking the chalice, he gave thanks. And he gave it to them, saying: "Drink from this, all of you. For this is my blood of the new covenant, which shall be shed for many as a remission of sins. But I say to you, I will not drink again from this fruit of the vine, until that day when I will drink it new with you in the kingdom of my Father.""

MATTHEW 26:26–29

"And while eating with them, Jesus took bread. And blessing it, he broke it and gave it to them, and he said: "Take. This is my body." And having taken the chalice, giving thanks, he gave it to them. And they all drank from it. And he said to them: "This is my blood of the new covenant, which shall be shed for many. Amen I say to you, that I will no longer drink from this fruit of the vine, until that day when I will drink it new in the kingdom of God.""

MARK 14:22–25

Fifth Luminous Mystery: The Institution of the Eucharist

FIRST SORROWFUL MYSTERY:

The Agony in the Garden

FRUIT OF THE MYSTERY: SORROW FOR SIN

_____
_____
_____
_____
_____
_____
_____

"THEN JESUS WENT WITH THEM TO A GARDEN, WHICH IS CALLED GETHSEMANI. AND HE SAID TO HIS DISCIPLES, "SIT DOWN HERE, WHILE I GO THERE AND PRAY." AND TAKING WITH HIM PETER AND THE TWO SONS OF ZEBEDEE, HE BEGAN TO BE SORROWFUL AND SADDENED. THEN HE SAID TO THEM: "MY SOUL IS SORROWFUL, EVEN UNTO DEATH. STAY HERE AND KEEP VIGIL WITH ME." AND CONTINUING ON A LITTLE FURTHER, HE FELL PROSTRATE ON HIS FACE, PRAYING AND SAYING: "MY FATHER, IF IT IS POSSIBLE, LET THIS CHALICE PASS AWAY FROM ME. YET TRULY, LET IT NOT BE AS I WILL, BUT AS YOU WILL." AND HE APPROACHED HIS DISCIPLES AND FOUND THEM SLEEPING. AND HE SAID TO PETER: "SO, WERE YOU NOT ABLE TO KEEP VIGIL WITH ME FOR ONE HOUR? BE VIGILANT AND PRAY, SO THAT YOU MAY NOT ENTER INTO TEMPTATION. INDEED, THE SPIRIT IS WILLING, BUT THE FLESH IS WEAK." AGAIN, A SECOND TIME, HE WENT AND PRAYED, SAYING, "MY FATHER, IF THIS CHALICE CANNOT PASS AWAY, UNLESS I DRINK IT, LET YOUR WILL BE DONE." AND AGAIN, HE WENT AND FOUND THEM SLEEPING, FOR THEIR EYES WERE HEAVY. AND LEAVING THEM BEHIND, AGAIN HE WENT AND PRAYED FOR THE THIRD TIME, SAYING THE SAME WORDS. THEN HE APPROACHED HIS DISCIPLES AND SAID TO THEM: "SLEEP NOW AND REST. BEHOLD, THE HOUR HAS DRAWN NEAR, AND THE SON OF MAN WILL BE DELIVERED INTO THE HANDS OF SINNERS."

MATTHEW 26:36-45

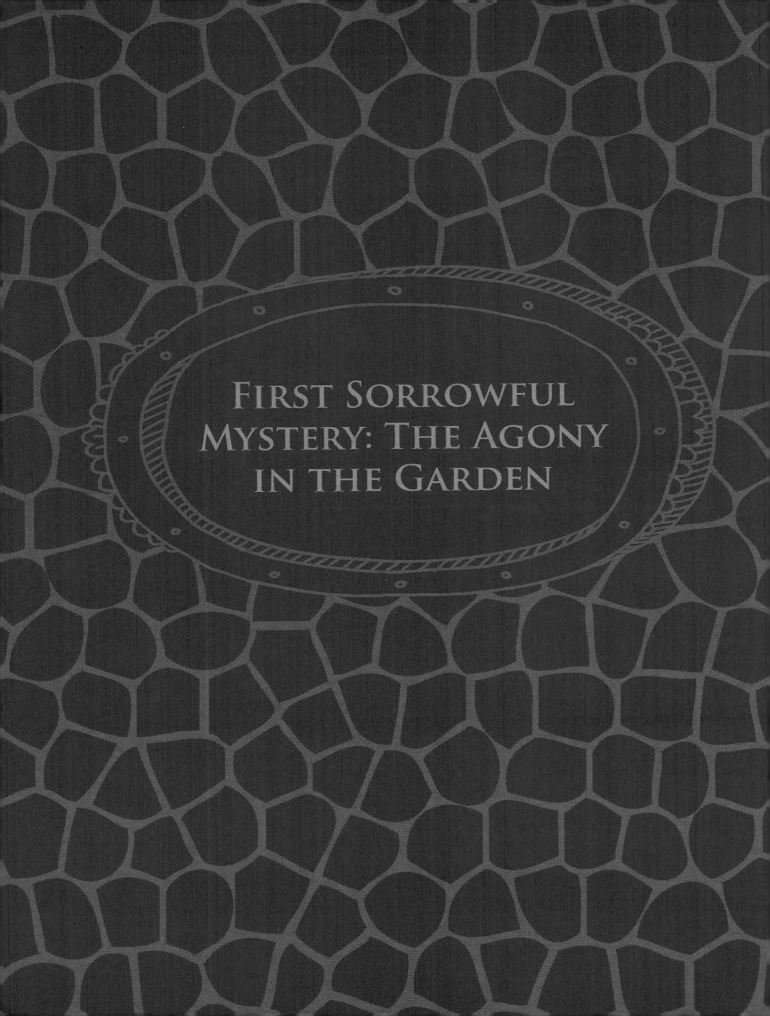

First Sorrowful Mystery: The Agony in the Garden

SECOND SORROWFUL MYSTERY:

The Scourging at the Pillar

FRUIT OF THE MYSTERY: MORTIFICATION & PURITY

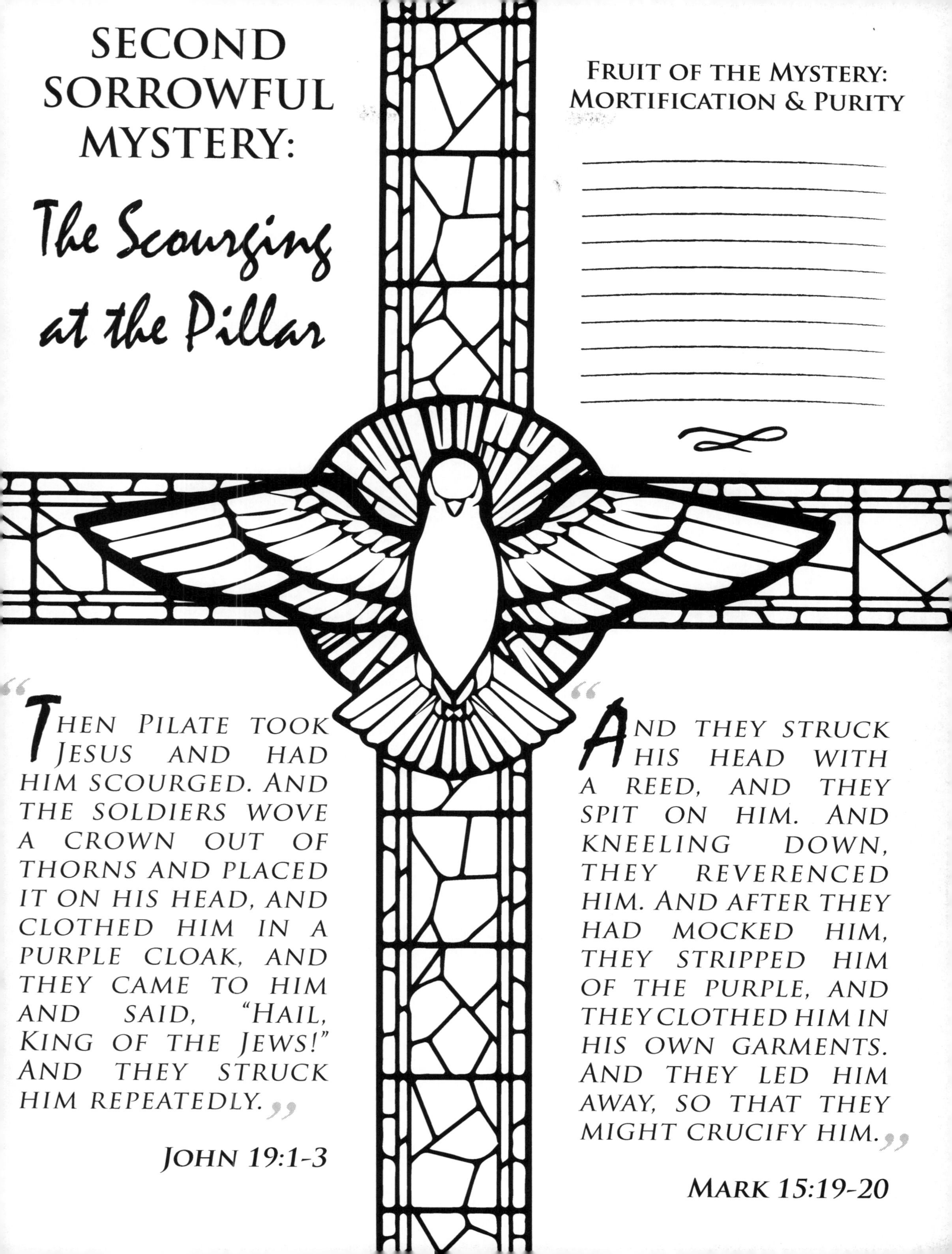

"THEN PILATE TOOK JESUS AND HAD HIM SCOURGED. AND THE SOLDIERS WOVE A CROWN OUT OF THORNS AND PLACED IT ON HIS HEAD, AND CLOTHED HIM IN A PURPLE CLOAK, AND THEY CAME TO HIM AND SAID, "HAIL, KING OF THE JEWS!" AND THEY STRUCK HIM REPEATEDLY."

JOHN 19:1-3

"AND THEY STRUCK HIS HEAD WITH A REED, AND THEY SPIT ON HIM. AND KNEELING DOWN, THEY REVERENCED HIM. AND AFTER THEY HAD MOCKED HIM, THEY STRIPPED HIM OF THE PURPLE, AND THEY CLOTHED HIM IN HIS OWN GARMENTS. AND THEY LED HIM AWAY, SO THAT THEY MIGHT CRUCIFY HIM."

MARK 15:19-20

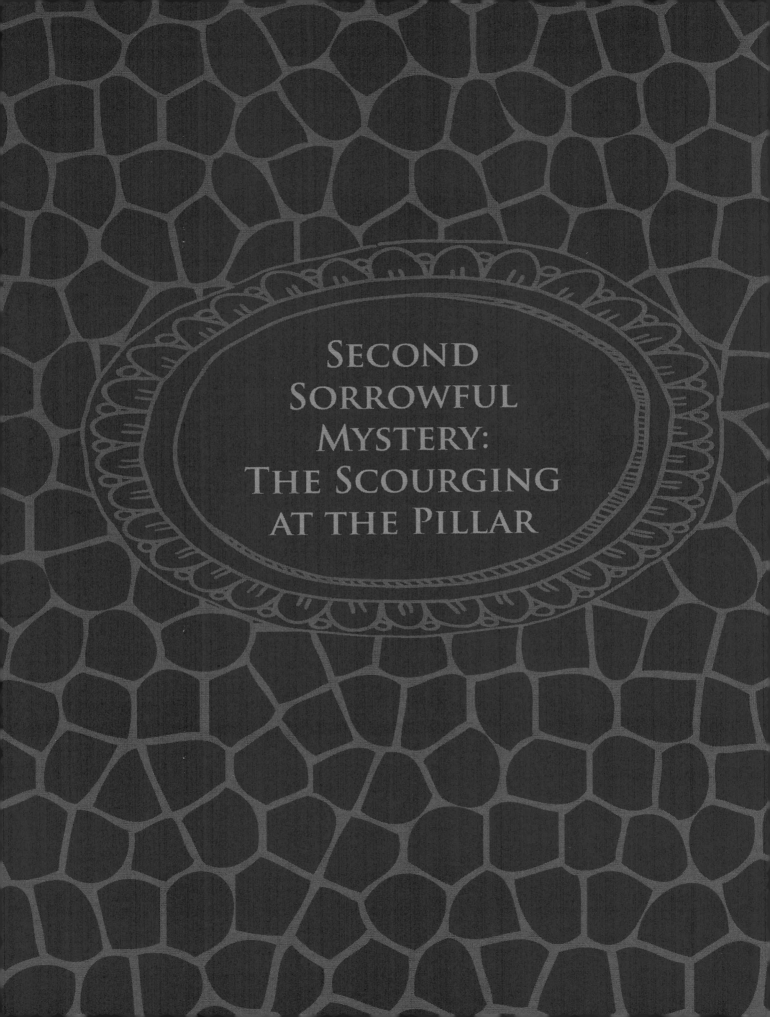

Second Sorrowful Mystery: The Scourging at the Pillar

THIRD SORROWFUL MYSTERY:

The Crowning with Thorns

"THEN THE SOLDIERS OF THE GOVERNOR TOOK JESUS INSIDE THE PRAETORIUM AND GATHERED THE WHOLE COHORT AROUND HIM. THEY STRIPPED OFF HIS CLOTHES AND THREW A SCARLET MILITARY CLOAK ABOUT HIM. WEAVING A CROWN OUT OF THORNS, THEY PLACED IT ON HIS HEAD, AND A REED IN HIS RIGHT HAND. AND KNEELING BEFORE HIM, THEY MOCKED HIM, SAYING, "HAIL, KING OF THE JEWS!" THEY SPAT UPON HIM AND TOOK THE REED AND KEPT STRIKING HIM ON THE HEAD. AND WHEN THEY HAD MOCKED HIM, THEY STRIPPED HIM OF THE CLOAK, DRESSED HIM IN HIS OWN CLOTHES, AND LED HIM OFF TO CRUCIFY HIM."

MATTHEW 27:27-31

"THEREFORE, PILATE THEN TOOK JESUS INTO CUSTODY AND SCOURGED HIM. AND THE SOLDIERS, PLAITING A CROWN OF THORNS, IMPOSED IT ON HIS HEAD. AND THEY PUT A PURPLE GARMENT AROUND HIM. AND THEY WERE APPROACHING HIM AND SAYING, "HAIL, KING OF THE JEWS!" AND THEY STRUCK HIM REPEATEDLY. THEN PILATE WENT OUTSIDE AGAIN, AND HE SAID TO THEM: "BEHOLD, I AM BRINGING HIM OUT TO YOU, SO THAT YOU MAY REALIZE THAT I FIND NO CASE AGAINST HIM." (THEN JESUS WENT OUT, BEARING THE CROWN OF THORNS AND THE PURPLE GARMENT.) AND HE SAID TO THEM, "BEHOLD THE MAN." THEREFORE, WHEN THE HIGH PRIESTS AND THE ATTENDANTS HAD SEEN HIM, THEY CRIED OUT, SAYING: "CRUCIFY HIM! CRUCIFY HIM!""

JOHN 19:1-6

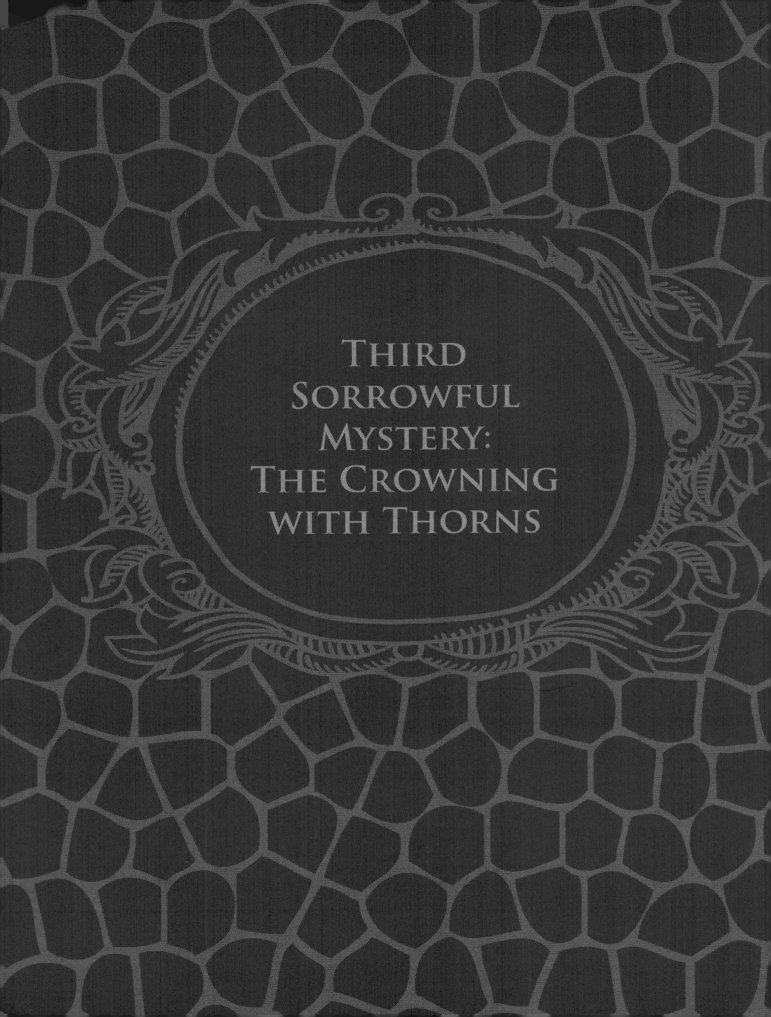

THIRD
SORROWFUL
MYSTERY:
THE CROWNING
WITH THORNS

FOURTH SORROWFUL MYSTERY:

The Carrying of the Cross

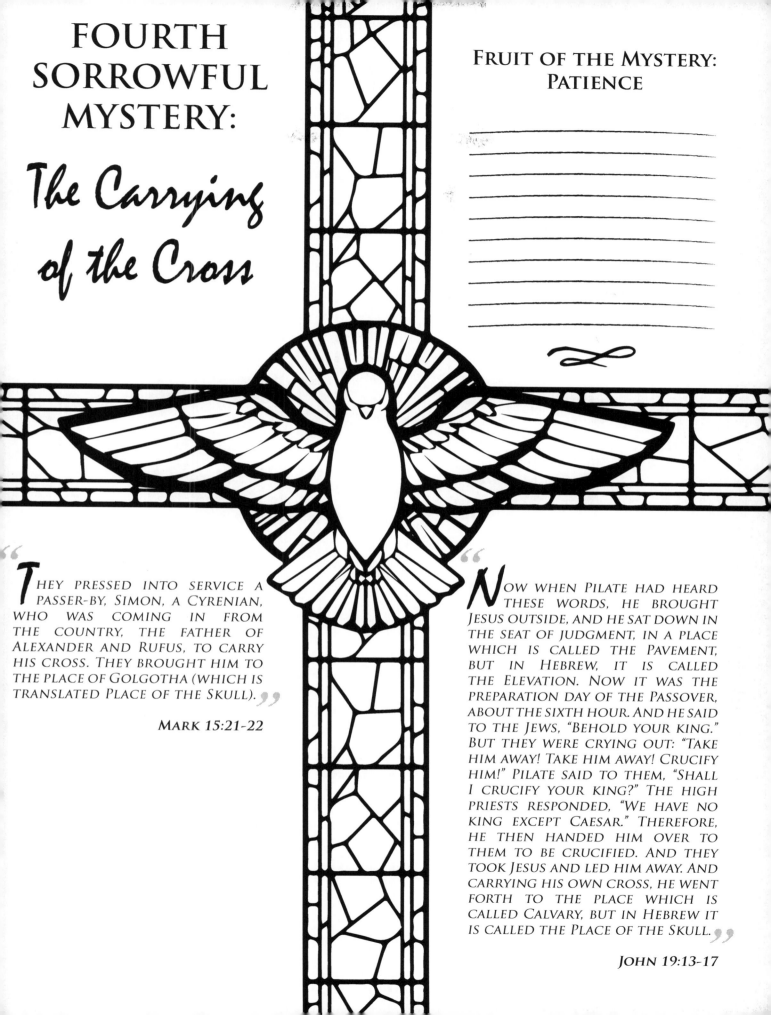

"THEY PRESSED INTO SERVICE A PASSER-BY, SIMON, A CYRENIAN, WHO WAS COMING IN FROM THE COUNTRY, THE FATHER OF ALEXANDER AND RUFUS, TO CARRY HIS CROSS. THEY BROUGHT HIM TO THE PLACE OF GOLGOTHA (WHICH IS TRANSLATED PLACE OF THE SKULL)."

MARK 15:21-22

"NOW WHEN PILATE HAD HEARD THESE WORDS, HE BROUGHT JESUS OUTSIDE, AND HE SAT DOWN IN THE SEAT OF JUDGMENT, IN A PLACE WHICH IS CALLED THE PAVEMENT, BUT IN HEBREW, IT IS CALLED THE ELEVATION. NOW IT WAS THE PREPARATION DAY OF THE PASSOVER, ABOUT THE SIXTH HOUR. AND HE SAID TO THE JEWS, "BEHOLD YOUR KING." BUT THEY WERE CRYING OUT: "TAKE HIM AWAY! TAKE HIM AWAY! CRUCIFY HIM!" PILATE SAID TO THEM, "SHALL I CRUCIFY YOUR KING?" THE HIGH PRIESTS RESPONDED, "WE HAVE NO KING EXCEPT CAESAR." THEREFORE, HE THEN HANDED HIM OVER TO THEM TO BE CRUCIFIED. AND THEY TOOK JESUS AND LED HIM AWAY. AND CARRYING HIS OWN CROSS, HE WENT FORTH TO THE PLACE WHICH IS CALLED CALVARY, BUT IN HEBREW IT IS CALLED THE PLACE OF THE SKULL."

JOHN 19:13-17

Fourth Sorrowful Mystery: The Carrying of the Cross

FIFTH SORROWFUL MYSTERY:

The Crucifixion and Death of our Lord

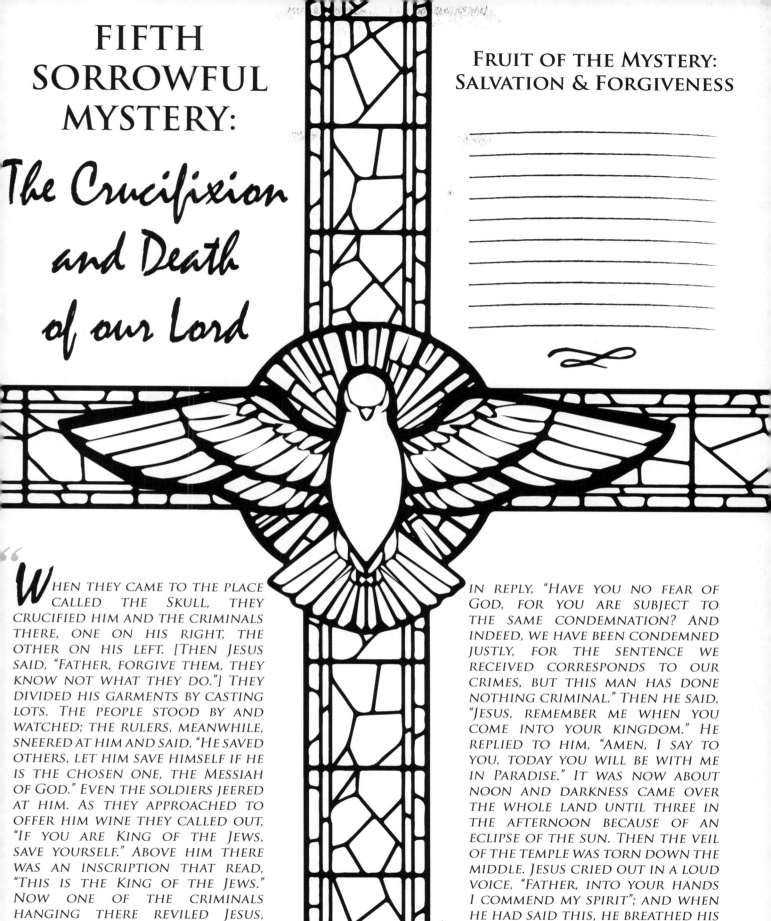

"When they came to the place called the Skull, they crucified him and the criminals there, one on his right, the other on his left. [Then Jesus said, "Father, forgive them, they know not what they do."] They divided his garments by casting lots. The people stood by and watched; the rulers, meanwhile, sneered at him and said, "He saved others, let him save himself if he is the chosen one, the Messiah of God." Even the soldiers jeered at him. As they approached to offer him wine they called out, "If you are King of the Jews, save yourself." Above him there was an inscription that read, "This is the King of the Jews." Now one of the criminals hanging there reviled Jesus, saying, "Are you not the Messiah? Save yourself and us." The other, however, rebuking him, said in reply, "Have you no fear of God, for you are subject to the same condemnation? And indeed, we have been condemned justly, for the sentence we received corresponds to our crimes, but this man has done nothing criminal." Then he said, "Jesus, remember me when you come into your kingdom." He replied to him, "Amen, I say to you, today you will be with me in Paradise." It was now about noon and darkness came over the whole land until three in the afternoon because of an eclipse of the sun. Then the veil of the temple was torn down the middle. Jesus cried out in a loud voice, "Father, into your hands I commend my spirit"; and when he had said this, he breathed his last."

Luke 23:33-46

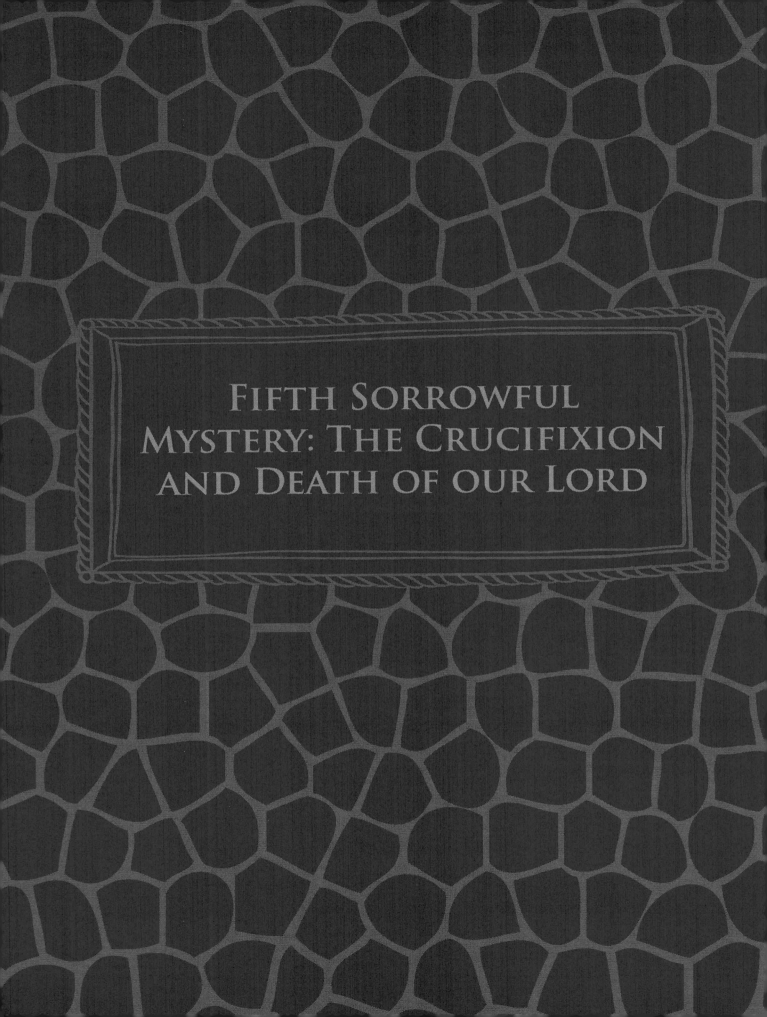

Fifth Sorrowful Mystery: The Crucifixion and Death of our Lord

FIRST GLORIOUS MYSTERY:

The Resurrection

"*But at daybreak on the first day of the week they took the spices they had prepared and went to the tomb. They found the stone rolled away from the tomb; but when they entered, they did not find the body of the Lord Jesus. While they were puzzling over this, behold, two men in dazzling garments appeared to them. They were terrified and bowed their faces to the ground. They said to them, "Why do you seek the living one among the dead?"*"

Luke 24:1-5

"*But Mary was standing outside the tomb, weeping. Then, while she was weeping, she bowed down and gazed into the tomb. And she saw two Angels in white, sitting where the body of Jesus had been placed, one at the head, and one at the feet. They said to her, "Woman, why are you weeping?" She said to them, "Because they have taken away my Lord, and I do not know where they have placed him." When she had said this, she turned around and saw Jesus standing there, but she did not know that it was Jesus. Jesus said to her: "Woman, why are you weeping? Who are you seeking?" Considering that it was the gardener, she said to him, "Sir, if you have moved him, tell me where you have placed him, and I will take him away." Jesus said to her, "Mary!" And turning, she said to him, "Rabboni!" (which means, Teacher).*"

John 20:11-16

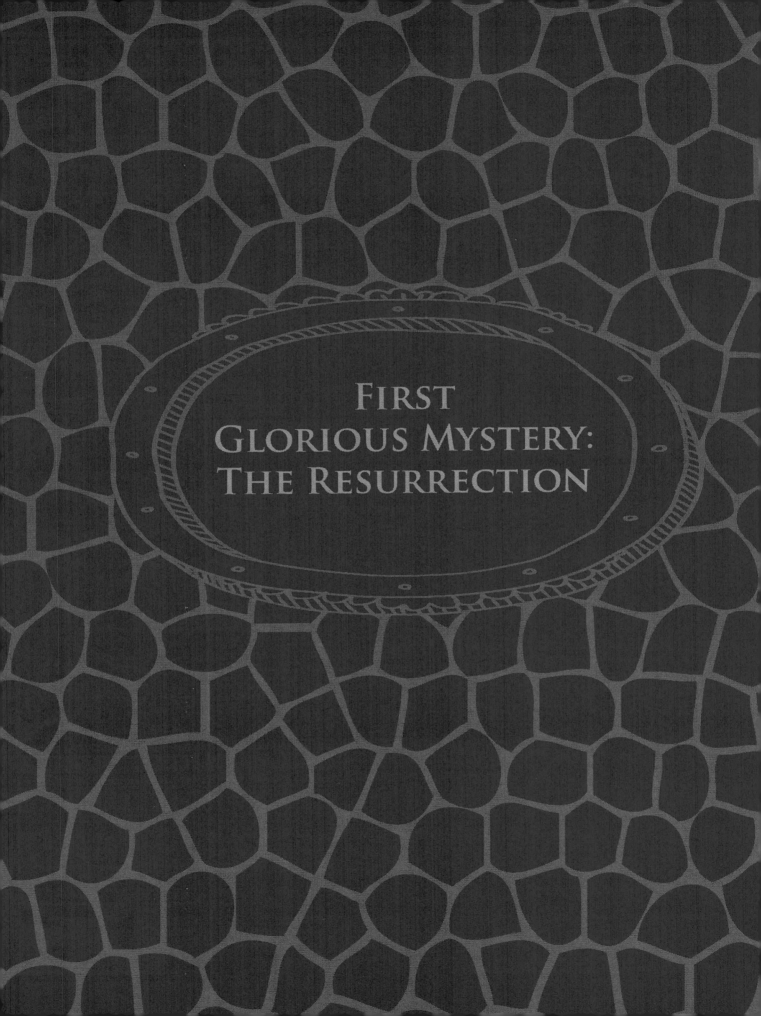

FIRST
GLORIOUS MYSTERY:
THE RESURRECTION

SECOND GLORIOUS MYSTERY:

The Ascension

FRUIT OF THE MYSTERY: HOPE & DESIRE FOR HEAVEN

_____
_____
_____
_____
_____
_____
_____
_____
_____
_____
_____
_____

"SO THEN THE LORD JESUS, AFTER HE SPOKE TO THEM, WAS TAKEN UP INTO HEAVEN AND TOOK HIS SEAT AT THE RIGHT HAND OF GOD."

MARK 16:19

"WHILE THEY WERE LOOKING INTENTLY AT THE SKY AS HE WAS GOING, SUDDENLY TWO MEN DRESSED IN WHITE GARMENTS STOOD BESIDE THEM. THEY SAID, "MEN OF GALILEE, WHY ARE YOU STANDING THERE LOOKING AT THE SKY? THIS JESUS WHO HAS BEEN TAKEN UP FROM YOU INTO HEAVEN WILL RETURN IN THE SAME WAY AS YOU HAVE SEEN HIM GOING INTO HEAVEN.""

ACTS 1:10-11

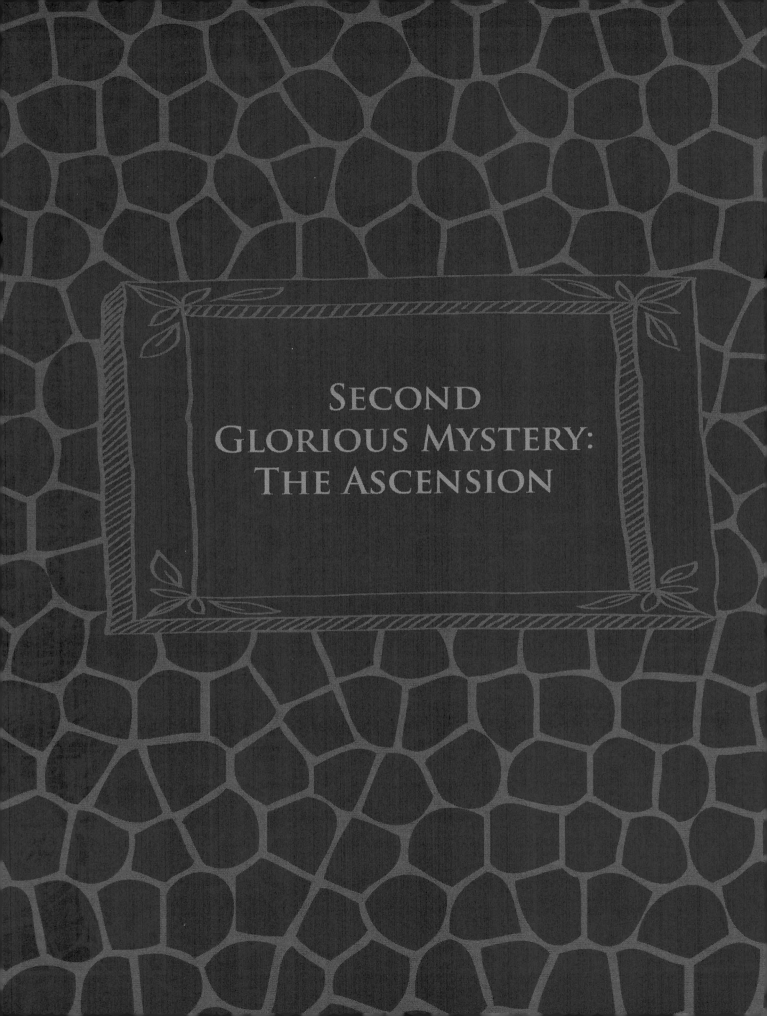

Second Glorious Mystery: The Ascension

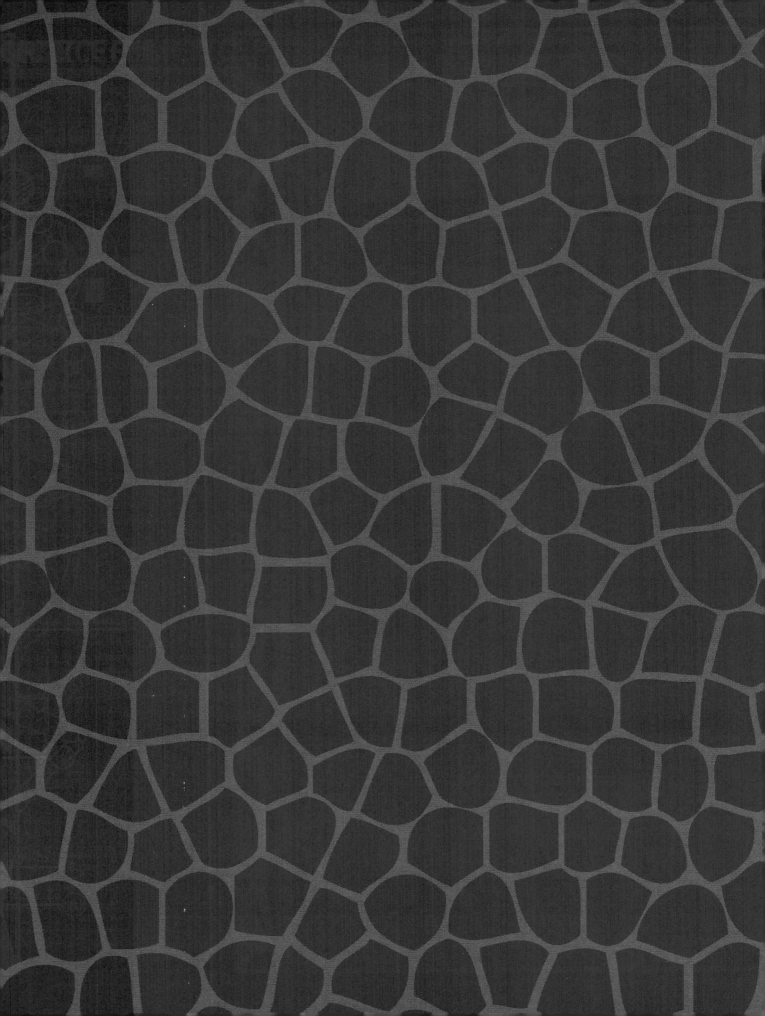

THIRD GLORIOUS MYSTERY:

The Descent of the Holy Spirit

FRUIT OF THE MYSTERY:
WISDOM & CHARITY

_____
_____
_____
_____
_____
_____
_____
_____
_____
_____

"And when the days of Pentecost were completed, they were all together in the same place. And suddenly, there came a sound from heaven, like that of a wind approaching violently, and it filled the entire house where they were sitting. And there appeared to them separate tongues, as if of fire, which settled upon each one of them. And they were all filled with the Holy Spirit. And they began to speak in various languages, just as the Holy Spirit bestowed eloquence to them. Now there were Jews staying in Jerusalem, pious men from every nation that is under heaven. And when this sound occurred, the multitude came together and was confused in mind, because each one was listening to them speaking in his own language. Then all were astonished, and they wondered, saying: "Behold, are not all of these who are speaking Galileans? And how is it that we have each heard them in our own language, into which we were born?"

ACTS 2:1-8

THIRD GLORIOUS MYSTERY: THE DESCENT OF THE HOLY SPIRIT

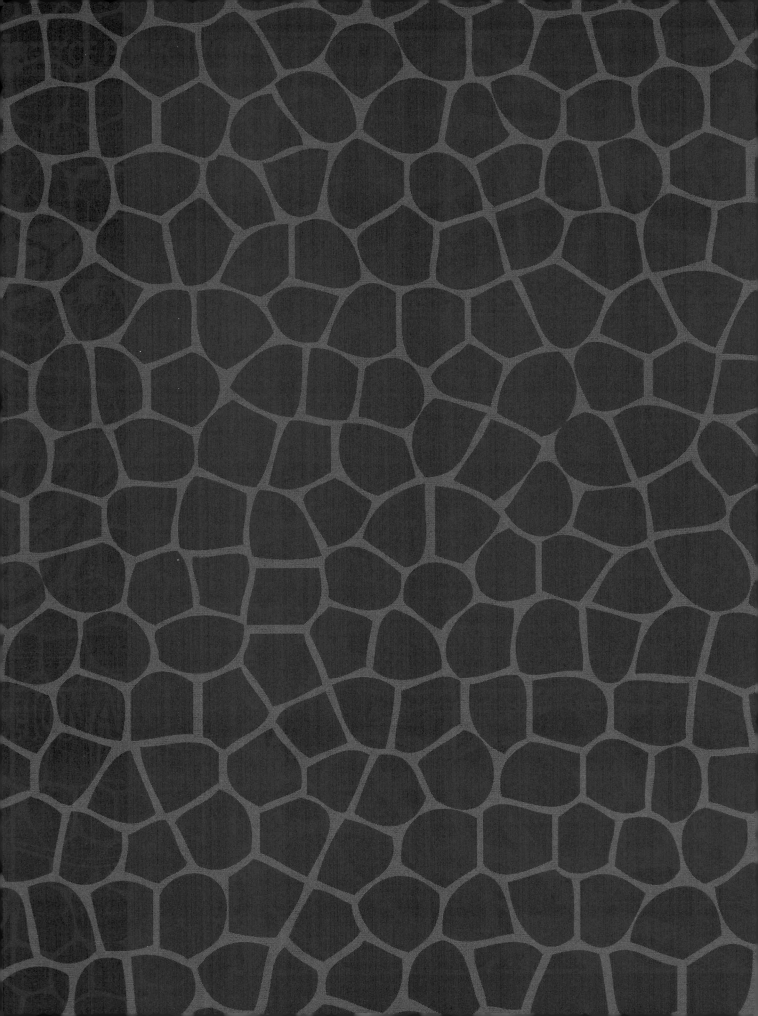

FOURTH GLORIOUS MYSTERY:

The Assumption of Mary

FRUIT OF THE MYSTERY: GRACE OF A HAPPY DEATH

"FOR HE HAS LOOKED UPON HIS HANDMAID'S LOWLINESS; BEHOLD, FROM NOW ON WILL ALL AGES CALL ME BLESSED. THE MIGHTY ONE HAS DONE GREAT THINGS FOR ME, AND HOLY IS HIS NAME."

LUKE 1: 48-49

"WE DO NOT WANT YOU TO BE UNAWARE, BROTHERS AND SISTERS, ABOUT THOSE WHO HAVE FALLEN ASLEEP. FOR IF WE BELIEVE THAT JESUS DIED AND ROSE, SO TOO WILL GOD, THROUGH JESUS, BRING WITH HIM THOSE WHO HAVE FALLEN ASLEEP. FOR THE LORD HIMSELF, WITH A WORD OF COMMAND, WITH THE VOICE OF AN ARCHANGEL AND WITH THE TRUMPET OF GOD, WILL COME DOWN FROM HEAVEN, AND THE DEAD IN CHRIST WILL RISE FIRST."

1 CORINTHIANS 15:20-23

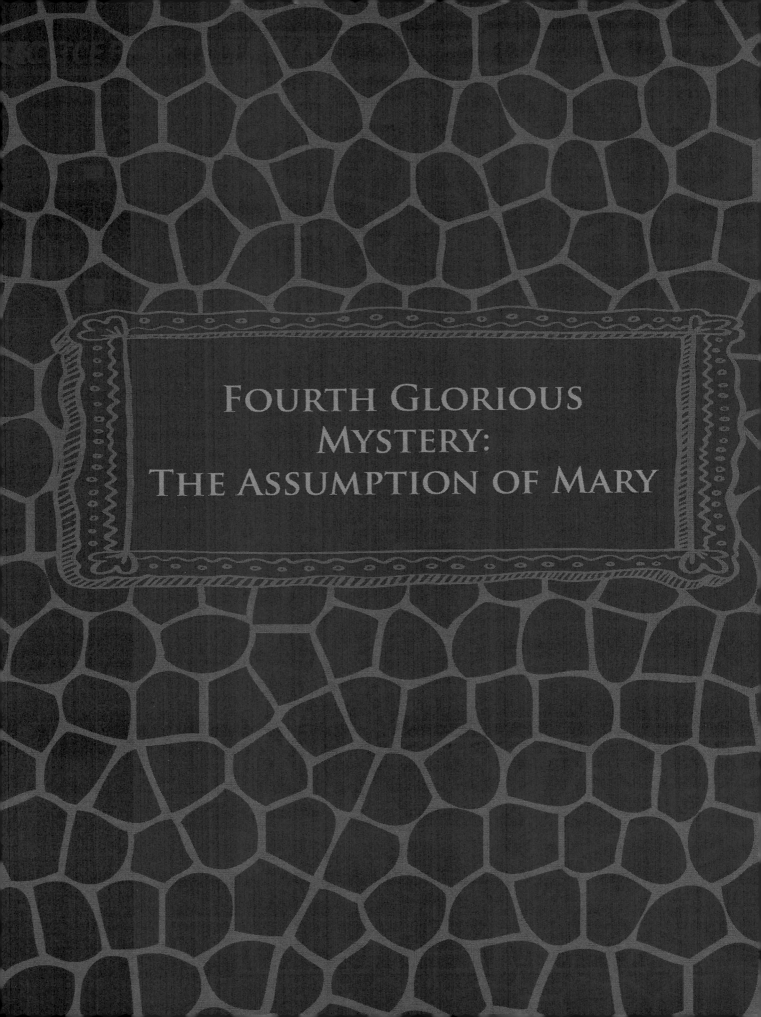

Fourth Glorious Mystery: The Assumption of Mary

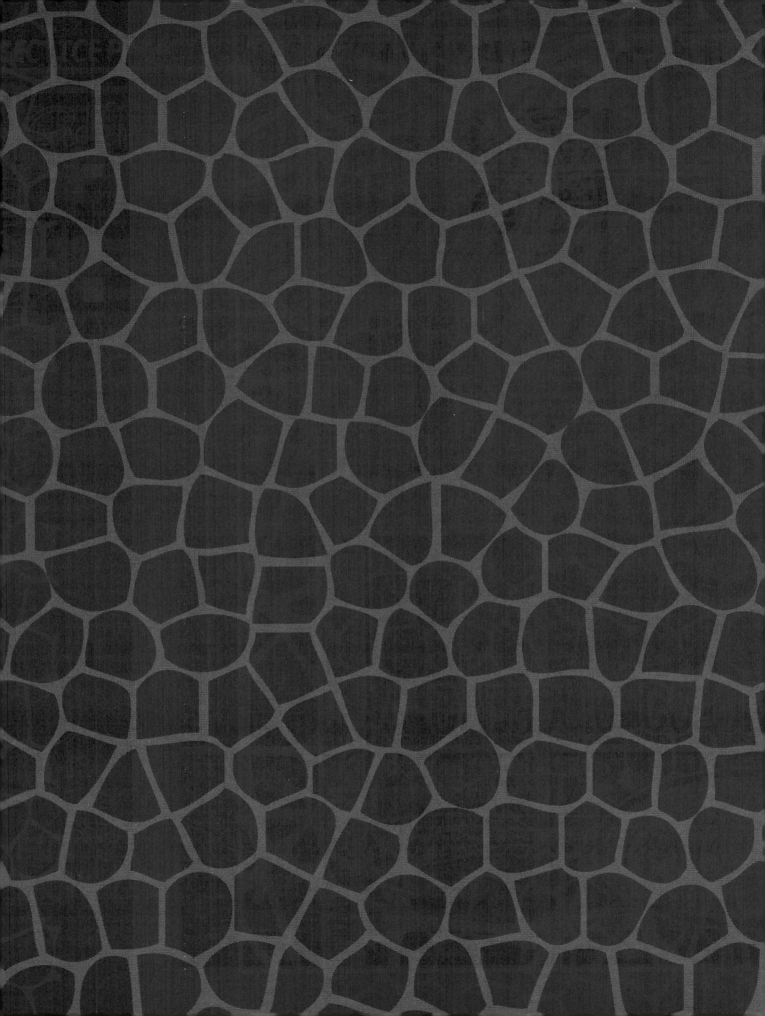

FIFTH GLORIOUS MYSTERY:

The Coronation of the Virgin

FRUIT OF THE MYSTERY: TRUST IN MARY'S INTERCESSION

_____
_____
_____
_____
_____
_____
_____
_____
_____
_____
_____

"I HAVE COMPETED WELL; I HAVE FINISHED THE RACE; I HAVE KEPT THE FAITH. FROM NOW ON THE CROWN OF RIGHTEOUSNESS AWAITS ME, WHICH THE LORD, THE JUST JUDGE, WILL AWARD TO ME ON THAT DAY, AND NOT ONLY FOR ME, BUT TO ALL WHO HAVE LONGED FOR HIS APPEARANCE."

2 TIMOTHY 4:7-8

"AND A GREAT SIGN APPEARED IN HEAVEN, A WOMAN CLOTHED WITH THE SUN, WITH THE MOON UNDER HER FEET, AND ON HER HEAD A CROWN OF TWELVE STARS; SHE WAS WITH CHILD AND SHE CRIED OUT IN HER PANGS OF BIRTH, IN ANGUISH FOR DELIVERY."

REVELATION 12:1-2

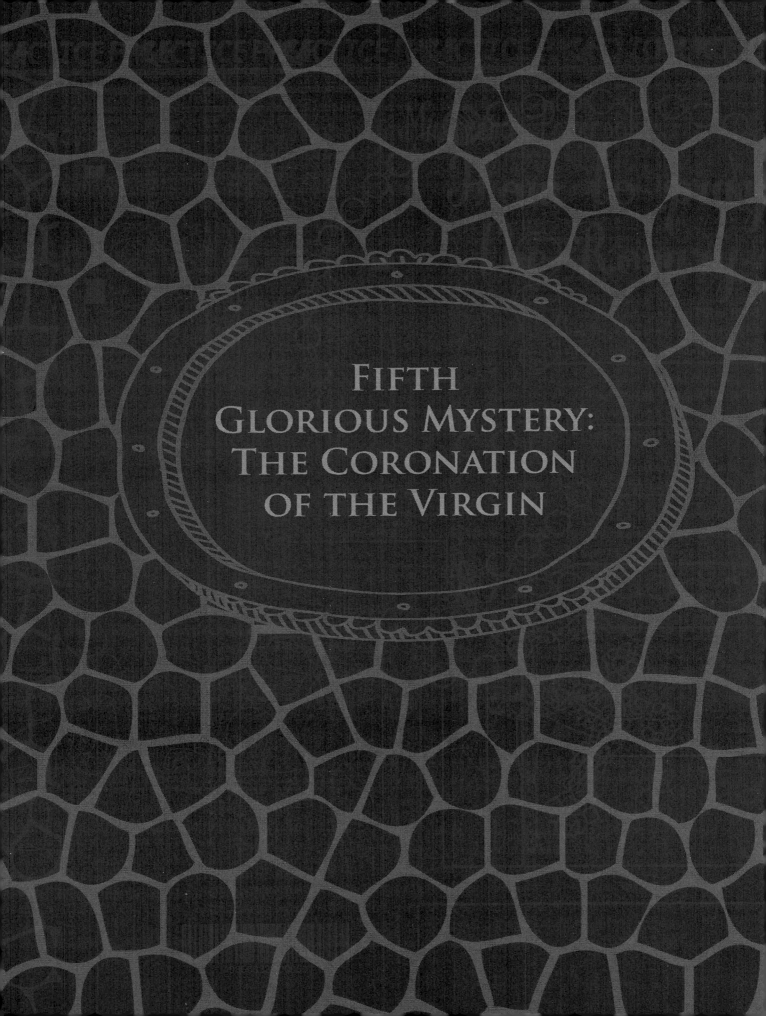

Fifth Glorious Mystery: The Coronation of the Virgin

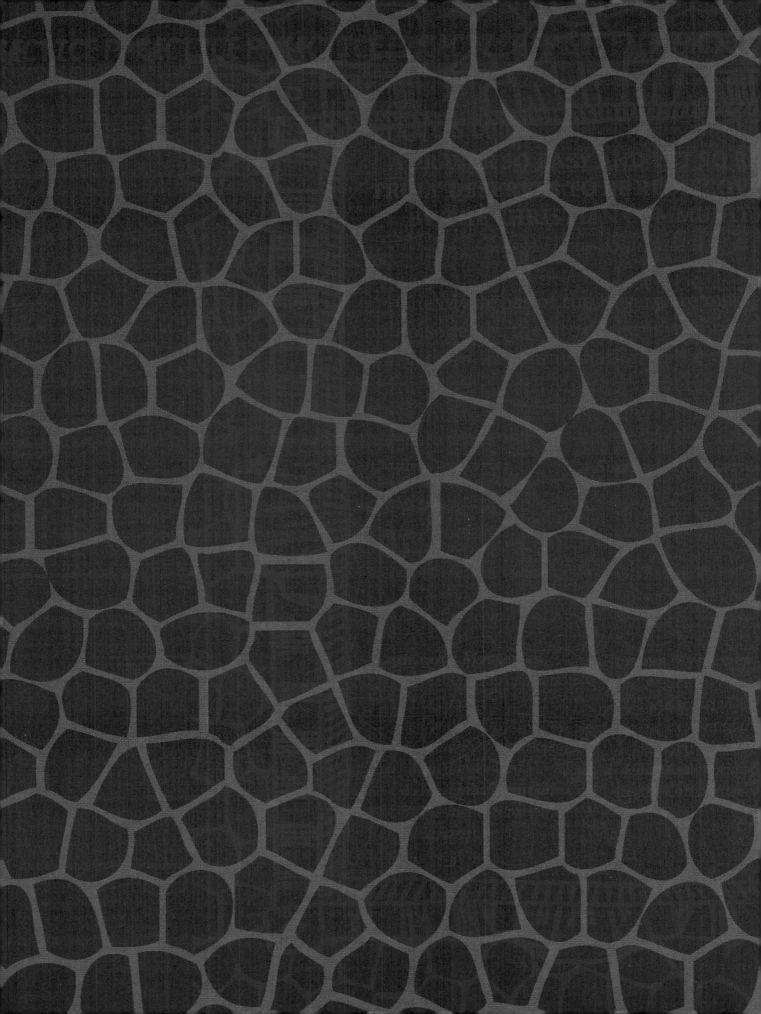

BE SURE TO FOLLOW US
ON SOCIAL MEDIA FOR THE
LATEST NEWS, SNEAK
PEEKS, & GIVEAWAYS

@drawntofaith

Drawn To Faith

@drawntofaith

ADD YOURSELF TO OUR MONTHLY
NEWSLETTER FOR FREE DIGITAL
DOWNLOADS AND DISCOUNT CODES
www.drawntofaith.com/newsletter

CHECK OUT OUR OTHER BOOKS!

www.drawntofaith.com

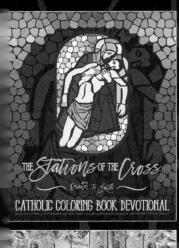

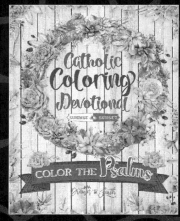

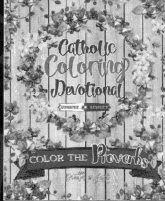

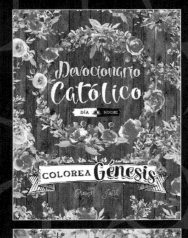

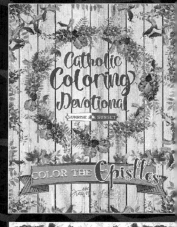

Printed in Great Britain
by Amazon

40856833R00059